·HOLIDAY·
COOKIES

Publications International, Ltd.

Let's get social!
 @Publications_International
 @PublicationsInternational
www.pilbooks.com

TABLE OF
CONTENTS

LOADED CHIPPERS

Triple-Chip Cookies

MAKES ABOUT 4 DOZEN COOKIES

2 cups old-fashioned oats
1⅓ cups all-purpose flour
¾ teaspoon baking soda
½ teaspoon baking powder
½ teaspoon salt
1 cup packed brown sugar
¾ cup (1½ sticks) unsalted butter, softened
¼ cup granulated sugar
1 egg

1 tablespoon honey
1 teaspoon vanilla
½ cup milk chocolate chips
½ cup white chocolate chips
½ cup semisweet chocolate chips
½ cup mini candy-coated chocolate pieces
½ cup chopped honey-roasted peanuts (optional)

1. Preheat oven to 350°F. Line cookie sheets with parchment paper.

2. Combine oats, flour, baking soda, baking powder and salt in medium bowl. Beat brown sugar, butter and granulated sugar in large bowl with electric mixer at medium-high speed until light and fluffy. Add egg, honey and vanilla; beat until well blended. Gradually add flour mixture at low speed, beating just until blended. Stir in chocolate chips, candies and peanuts, if desired. Drop dough by tablespoonfuls about 2 inches apart onto prepared cookie sheets.

3. Bake 12 to 14 minutes or until puffed and golden. Cool on cookie sheets 5 minutes. Remove to wire racks; cool completely.

White Chocolate Biggies

2½ cups all-purpose flour
⅔ cup unsweetened cocoa powder
1 teaspoon baking soda
1 teaspoon salt
1½ cups (3 sticks) unsalted butter, softened
1 cup granulated sugar
¾ cup packed brown sugar
2 eggs
2 teaspoons vanilla
1 package (10 ounces) large white chocolate chips *or* 2 bars (about 4 ounces each) white chocolate, cut into pieces
¾ cup pecan halves, coarsely chopped
½ cup golden raisins

1. Preheat oven to 350°F. Lightly grease cookie sheets or line with parchment paper. Combine flour, cocoa, baking soda and salt in medium bowl.

2. Beat butter, granulated sugar and brown sugar in large bowl with electric mixer at medium-high speed until light and fluffy. Add eggs and vanilla; beat until well blended. Gradually add flour mixture at low speed, beating just until blended. Stir in white chocolate chips, pecans and raisins.

3. Drop dough by ⅓ cupfuls about 4 inches apart onto prepared cookie sheets. Press each cookie to flatten slightly.

4. Bake 12 to 14 minutes or until firm in center. Cool on cookie sheets 5 minutes. Remove to wire racks; cool completely.

One-Bite Chocolate Chip Cookies

1¼ cups all-purpose flour
½ teaspoon baking soda
¼ teaspoon salt
½ cup (1 stick) unsalted butter, softened
½ cup packed brown sugar

¼ cup granulated sugar
1 egg
1 teaspoon vanilla
1¼ cups mini semisweet chocolate chips
Sea salt (optional)

1. Preheat oven to 350°F. Combine flour, baking soda and salt in medium bowl.

2. Beat butter, brown sugar and granulated sugar in large bowl with electric mixer at medium-high speed until light and fluffy. Beat in egg and vanilla until blended. Gradually add flour mixture at low speed, beating just until blended. Stir in chocolate chips.

3. Drop dough by ½ teaspoonfuls 1 inch apart onto ungreased cookie sheets. Sprinkle very lightly with sea salt, if desired.

4. Bake 6 minutes or just until edges are golden brown. (Centers of cookies will be very light and will not look done.) Cool on cookie sheets 2 minutes. Remove to wire racks; cool completely.

Ultimate White Chocolate Chippers

1¼ cups all-purpose flour
½ teaspoon baking soda
¼ teaspoon salt
½ cup (1 stick) unsalted butter, softened
½ cup packed brown sugar
¼ cup granulated sugar
1 egg

1½ teaspoons vanilla
1 cup white chocolate chips
¾ cup coarsely chopped pecans, toasted*

To toast pecans, place in single layer on ungreased baking sheet. Bake in preheated 350°F oven 8 to 10 minutes or until lightly browned, stirring occasionally. Cool before using.

1. Preheat oven to 375°F. Combine flour, baking soda and salt in medium bowl.

2. Beat butter, brown sugar and granulated sugar in large bowl with electric mixer at medium-high speed until light and fluffy. Add egg and vanilla; beat until well blended. Gradually add flour mixture at low speed, beating just until blended. Stir in chips and pecans.

3. Drop dough by heaping teaspoonfuls 2 inches apart onto ungreased cookie sheets.

4. Bake 8 to 10 minutes or until edges are golden brown. Cool on cookie sheets 2 minutes. Remove to wire racks; cool completely.

Flourless Peanut Butter Chocolate Chippers

1 cup packed brown sugar
1 cup creamy or chunky peanut butter*
1 egg

Granulated sugar
½ cup milk chocolate chips
*Do not use natural peanut butter.

1. Preheat oven to 350°F.

2. Beat brown sugar, peanut butter and egg in medium bowl with electric mixer at medium speed until well blended.

3. Shape dough into 1½-inch balls. Place 2 inches apart on ungreased cookie sheets. Dip fork into granulated sugar; flatten each ball to ½-inch thickness, crisscrossing with fork. Press 3 to 4 chocolate chips on top of each cookie.

4. Bake 12 minutes or until just set. Cool on cookie sheets 2 minutes. Remove to wire racks; cool completely.

Chocolate Chip Peanut Butter Cookies

1⅓ cups all-purpose flour
½ teaspoon salt
½ teaspoon baking soda
½ cup (1 stick) unsalted butter, softened
½ cup creamy peanut butter
½ cup granulated sugar

¼ cup packed brown sugar
1 egg
1 teaspoon vanilla
1 cup semisweet chocolate chips
½ cup peanuts

1. Preheat oven to 350°F. Lightly grease cookie sheets or line with parchment paper. Combine flour, salt and baking soda in medium bowl.

2. Beat butter, peanut butter, granulated sugar and brown sugar in large bowl with electric mixer at medium speed until light and fluffy. Add egg and vanilla; beat until well blended. Gradually add flour mixture at low speed, beating just until blended. Stir in chocolate chips and peanuts.

3. Drop dough by rounded tablespoonfuls 2 inches apart onto prepared cookie sheets.

4. Bake 12 minutes or until edges are lightly browned. Cool on cookie sheets 2 minutes. Remove to wire racks; cool completely.

Super Chip Cookies

1¼ cups all-purpose flour

2 tablespoons unsweetened cocoa powder

½ teaspoon salt

½ teaspoon baking soda

½ cup (1 stick) unsalted butter, softened

½ cup granulated sugar

¼ cup packed brown sugar

1 egg

1 teaspoon vanilla

⅓ cup *each* white chocolate chips and semisweet chocolate chips

¼ cup *each* peanut butter chips and milk chocolate chips

1. Preheat oven to 350°F. Lightly grease cookie sheets or line with parchment paper. Combine flour, cocoa, salt and baking soda in medium bowl.

2. Beat butter, granulated sugar and brown sugar in large bowl with electric mixer at medium-high speed 3 minutes or until light and fluffy. Add egg and vanilla; beat until well blended. Gradually add flour mixture at low speed, beating just until blended. Stir in all chips.

3. Drop dough by rounded tablespoonfuls 2 inches apart onto prepared cookie sheets.

4. Bake 10 to 11 minutes or until set and no longer shiny. Cool on cookie sheets 2 minutes. Remove to wire racks; cool completely.

Macadamia Chippers

1½ cups all-purpose flour
½ teaspoon salt
¼ teaspoon baking soda
⅔ cup shortening *or*
    10 tablespoons unsalted
    butter, softened
1½ cups packed brown sugar

2 eggs
1 teaspoon vanilla
1 cup white chocolate chips or
    butterscotch chips
1 cup macadamia nuts, coarsely
    chopped

1. Preheat oven to 375°F. Combine flour, salt and baking soda in medium bowl.

2. Beat shortening and brown sugar in large bowl with electric mixer at medium-high speed until light and fluffy. Add eggs and vanilla; beat until well blended. Gradually add flour mixture at low speed, beating just until blended. Stir in chips and nuts.

3. Drop dough by rounded tablespoonfuls 2 inches apart onto ungreased cookie sheets.

4. Bake 9 to 11 minutes or until cookies are set. Cool on cookie sheets 2 minutes. Remove to wire racks; cool completely.

Loaded Oatmeal Cookies

1½ cups quick or old-fashioned oats

1 cup all-purpose flour

½ teaspoon baking soda

½ teaspoon salt

½ teaspoon ground cinnamon

1 cup packed brown sugar

¾ cup (1½ sticks) unsalted butter, softened

1 egg

1 tablespoon milk

1 teaspoon vanilla

1 cup semisweet chocolate chips

1 cup butterscotch chips

¾ cup raisins

½ cup chopped walnuts

1. Preheat oven to 350°F. Combine oats, flour, baking soda, salt and cinnamon in medium bowl.

2. Beat brown sugar and butter in large bowl with electric mixer at medium-high speed until creamy. Beat in egg, milk and vanilla until light and fluffy. Gradually add oat mixture at low speed, beating just until blended. Stir in chocolate chips, butterscotch chips, raisins and walnuts.

3. Drop dough by rounded tablespoonfuls 2 inches apart onto ungreased cookie sheets.

4. Bake 12 to 15 minutes or until edges are lightly browned. Cool on cookie sheets 2 minutes. Remove to wire racks; cool completely.

Whole Grain Chippers

1 cup (2 sticks) unsalted butter, softened
1 cup packed brown sugar
2/3 cup granulated sugar
2 eggs
1 teaspoon vanilla
1 teaspoon baking soda

1 teaspoon salt
2 cups old-fashioned oats
1 cup all-purpose flour
1 cup whole wheat flour
1 package (12 ounces) semisweet chocolate chips
1 cup sunflower seeds

1. Preheat oven to 375°F. Grease cookie sheets or line with parchment paper.

2. Beat butter, brown sugar and granulated sugar in large bowl with electric mixer at medium-high speed until light and fluffy. Beat in eggs and vanilla until well blended. Add baking soda and salt; beat until blended. Add oats, all-purpose flour and whole wheat flour at low speed to make stiff dough. Stir in chocolate chips.

3. Place sunflower seeds in shallow bowl. Shape rounded teaspoonfuls of dough into balls; roll in sunflower seeds. Place 2 inches apart on prepared cookie sheets.

4. Bake 8 to 10 minutes or until firm and lightly browned. *Do not overbake.* Cool on cookie sheets 2 minutes. Remove to wire racks; cool completely.

Little Butterscotch Candy Cookies

½ cup granulated sugar
3 tablespoons canola or
  vegetable oil
1 egg
2 tablespoons molasses
1 teaspoon vanilla

1 cup old-fashioned oats
⅔ cup all-purpose flour
1½ teaspoons ground cinnamon
½ teaspoon baking soda
¼ teaspoon salt
½ cup butterscotch chips

1. Preheat oven to 375°F. Line two cookie sheets with parchment paper.

2. Combine sugar and oil in medium bowl; stir about 30 seconds or until well blended (mixture will resemble small peas). Add egg, molasses and vanilla; mix well. Add oats, flour, cinnamon, baking soda and salt; stir until well blended. Add butterscotch chips; mix well.

3. Drop batter by teaspoonfuls onto prepared cookie sheets. Coat fork with nonstick cooking spray; gently flatten each cookie.

4. Bake 2½ minutes for chewy texture or 3 minutes for cake-like texture. Do not overbake; cookies will not look done. Cool on cookie sheets 1 minute. Remove to wire rack; cool completely.

Ultimate Chippers

2½ cups all-purpose flour
1 teaspoon baking soda
½ teaspoon salt
1 cup (2 sticks) unsalted butter, softened
1 cup packed brown sugar
½ cup granulated sugar

2 eggs
1 tablespoon vanilla
1 cup semisweet chocolate chips
1 cup milk chocolate chips
1 cup white chocolate chips

1. Preheat oven to 375°F. Combine flour, baking soda and salt in medium bowl.

2. Beat butter, brown sugar and granulated sugar in large bowl with electric mixer at medium-high speed until light and fluffy. Beat in eggs and vanilla. Gradually add flour mixture at low speed, beating just until blended. Stir in all chips.

3. Drop dough by heaping teaspoonfuls 2 inches apart onto ungreased cookie sheets.

4. Bake 10 to 12 minutes or until edges are golden brown. Cool on cookie sheets 2 minutes. Remove to wire racks; cool completely.

DECADENT CHOCOLATE DELIGHTS

Chocolate Cinnamon Macaroons

8 ounces semisweet chocolate, divided

1¾ cups plus ⅓ cup whole almonds, divided

¾ cup granulated sugar

½ teaspoon salt

2 egg whites

1 teaspoon ground cinnamon

1 teaspoon vanilla

1. Preheat oven to 400°F. Grease cookie sheets or line with parchment paper.

2. Place 5 ounces of chocolate in food processor; process until coarsely chopped. Add 1¾ cups almonds, sugar and salt; process using on/off pulses until mixture is finely ground. Add egg whites, cinnamon and vanilla; process just until mixture forms moist dough.

3. Shape dough into 1-inch balls. (Dough will be sticky.) Place 2 inches apart on prepared cookie sheets. Press 1 whole almond into center of each dough ball.

4. Bake 8 to 10 minutes or just until set. Cool on cookie sheets 2 minutes. Remove to wire racks; cool completely.

5. Melt remaining 3 ounces of chocolate. Place in small resealable food storage bag. Cut off small corner of bag. Drizzle chocolate over cookies. Let stand until set.

Holiday Buttons

2 cups all-purpose flour
¼ teaspoon salt
⅛ teaspoon baking powder
½ cup (1 stick) unsalted butter, softened
1¼ cups chocolate-hazelnut spread, divided

⅓ cup granulated sugar
⅓ cup packed brown sugar
1 egg
½ teaspoon almond extract
Decors, nonpareils or decorating sugar

1. Combine flour, salt and baking powder in medium bowl. Beat butter, ½ cup chocolate-hazelnut spread, granulated sugar and brown sugar in large bowl with electric mixer at medium speed until well blended. Add egg and almond extract; beat until well blended. Gradually add flour mixture at low speed, beating just until blended. Divide dough into four pieces; shape each piece into 7-inch log. Wrap in plastic wrap; refrigerate 2 to 3 hours or until firm.

2. Preheat oven to 325°F. Grease cookie sheets or line with parchment paper. Cut dough into ⅜-inch-thick slices; place 1 inch apart on prepared cookie sheets. Poke four holes in each slice with straw.

3. Bake 12 to 14 minutes or until cookies are set. Cool on cookie sheets 1 minute. Remove to wire racks; cool completely.

4. Spread 1 teaspoon chocolate-hazelnut spread on flat sides of half of cookies; top with remaining cookies. Roll edges of cookies in decors.

Cocoa Meringue Kisses

MAKES 9 DOZEN COOKIES

½ cup raw hazelnuts
1 cup granulated sugar, divided
5 tablespoons cocoa powder
3 tablespoons cornstarch
½ teaspoon ground cinnamon
¼ teaspoon grated nutmeg

3 egg whites, at room temperature
¼ teaspoon cream of tartar
1¼ teaspoons vanilla
3 ounces bittersweet chocolate, finely chopped

1. Preheat oven to 350°F. Place hazelnuts in small baking pan; bake 15 to 18 minutes or until skins split and nuts are golden. Transfer nuts to clean kitchen towel; rub nuts in towel to remove most of skins. Position racks in upper and lower thirds of oven. *Reduce oven temperature to 200°F.* Line two cookie sheets with foil.

2. Place hazelnuts and ⅓ cup sugar in food processor; process with on/off pulses about 2 minutes or until nuts are finely ground. Add cocoa, cornstarch, cinnamon and nutmeg; pulse until blended.

3. Beat egg whites in large bowl with electric mixer at medium-high speed until foamy. Add cream of tartar; beat until egg whites hold soft peaks. Gradually add remaining ⅔ cup sugar, beating until egg whites hold firm and shiny, but not stiff, peaks. Stir in vanilla.

4. Fold hazelnut mixture into beaten egg whites in three parts, mixing well after each addition. Scoop 1-inch mounds 1 inch apart onto prepared cookie sheets with spoon.

5. Bake 45 minutes. Rotate cookie sheets top to bottom and front to back; bake 45 minutes. Turn oven off; leave meringues in oven 1 hour. Carefully peel meringues from foil and turn bottoms up.

6. Place chocolate in small microwavable bowl; microwave on LOW (30%) 30 seconds. Stir chocolate; microwave at additional 15-second intervals until melted, stirring frequently. Use pastry brush to coat bottoms of meringues with melted chocolate. Refrigerate 10 minutes to set chocolate. Warm remaining melted chocolate in microwave; brush bottom of meringues again with melted chocolate. Refrigerate 10 minutes to set. Store meringues tightly covered with foil up to 1 week.

Dark Cocoa Spice Cookies

2½ cups all-purpose flour

½ cup unsweetened Dutch process cocoa powder

1 teaspoon ground cinnamon

1 teaspoon ground cardamom

½ teaspoon baking soda

½ teaspoon salt

1½ cups packed dark brown sugar

1 cup (2 sticks) unsalted butter, softened

2 egg yolks

1 teaspoon vanilla

Demerara sugar or coarse decorating sugar

1. Whisk flour, cocoa, cinnamon, cardamom, baking soda and salt in medium bowl. Beat brown sugar and butter in large bowl with electric mixer at medium speed until light and fluffy. Beat in egg yolks and vanilla. Gradually add flour mixture at low speed, beating just until blended.

2. Spread demerara sugar evenly on waxed paper. Divide dough into four pieces; shape each piece into 6-inch log. Roll logs in sugar, coating evenly. Wrap in plastic wrap and refrigerate 3 to 4 hours or until firm.

3. Preheat oven to 325°F. Line cookie sheets with parchment paper. Cut each log into 16 slices; place 1 inch apart on prepared cookie sheets.

4. Bake 12 minutes. Cool on cookie sheets 5 minutes. Remove to wire racks; cool completely.

Chocolate Malted Cookies

½ cup (1 stick) unsalted butter, softened

½ cup shortening

1¾ cups powdered sugar, divided

1 teaspoon vanilla

2 cups all-purpose flour

1 cup malted milk powder, divided

¼ cup unsweetened cocoa powder

½ teaspoon salt

1. Beat butter, shortening, ¾ cup powdered sugar and vanilla in large bowl. Add flour, ½ cup malted milk powder, cocoa and salt; beat until well blended. Refrigerate several hours or overnight.

2. Preheat oven to 350°F. Shape slightly mounded teaspoonfuls of dough into balls; place about 2 inches apart on ungreased cookie sheets. Bake 14 to 16 minutes or until lightly browned.

3. Meanwhile, combine remaining 1 cup powdered sugar and ½ cup malted milk powder in medium bowl. Remove cookies to wire racks; cool 5 minutes. Roll cookies in powdered sugar mixture.

TIP: For chocolate-covered cookies, substitute 6 ounces melted semisweet chocolate for the 1 cup powdered sugar and ½ cup malted milk powder. Dip cookies in melted chocolate and let stand on wire racks until coating is set.

Cocoa Crackles

1½ cups all-purpose flour

⅓ cup unsweetened cocoa powder

½ teaspoon salt

½ teaspoon baking soda

½ cup (1 stick) unsalted butter, softened

½ cup granulated sugar

¼ cup packed brown sugar

2 eggs

1 teaspoon vanilla

Powdered sugar

1. Preheat oven to 350°F. Grease cookie sheets or line with parchment paper. Combine flour, cocoa, salt and baking soda in medium bowl.

2. Beat butter, granulated sugar and brown sugar in large bowl with electric mixer until light and fluffy. Add eggs and vanilla; beat until well blended. Add flour mixture; beat just until blended.

3. Place powdered sugar in shallow bowl. Shape dough by heaping teaspoonfuls into balls. Roll balls in powdered sugar; place 2 inches apart on prepared cookie sheets.

4. Bake about 11 minutes or until set and no longer shiny. Cool on cookie sheets 2 minutes. Remove to wire racks; cool completely.

Dark Chocolate Dreams

½ cup all-purpose flour

¾ teaspoon espresso powder *or* ¼ teaspoon ground cinnamon

½ teaspoon baking powder

½ teaspoon salt

16 ounces bittersweet chocolate, coarsely chopped

¼ cup (½ stick) unsalted butter

1½ cups granulated sugar

3 eggs

1 teaspoon vanilla

1 package (12 ounces) white chocolate chips

1 cup dark chocolate chips or chopped toasted pecans

1. Preheat oven to 350°F. Grease cookie sheets or line with parchment paper. Combine flour, espresso powder, baking powder and salt in small bowl.

2. Combine chopped chocolate and butter in large microwavable bowl. Microwave on HIGH 2 minutes; stir. Microwave 1 to 2 minutes, stirring after 1 minute, or until chocolate is melted. Cool slightly.

3. Beat sugar, eggs and vanilla with electric mixer at medium-high speed about 6 minutes or until very thick and mixture turns pale color. Reduce speed to low; gradually beat in chocolate mixture until well blended. Gradually beat in flour mixture until blended. Fold in white chocolate chips and dark chocolate chips.

4. Drop dough by level ⅓ cupfuls 3 inches apart onto prepared cookie sheets. Flatten into 4-inch circles with moistened fingers.

5. Bake 12 minutes or just until firm and surface begins to crack. *Do not overbake.* Cool cookies on cookie sheets 5 minutes. Remove to wire racks; cool completely.

Chocolate Toffee Giants

½ cup all-purpose flour
¼ teaspoon baking powder
¼ teaspoon salt
1 package (12 ounces) semisweet chocolate chips, divided
¼ cup (½ stick) unsalted butter, cut into small pieces

¾ cup packed brown sugar
2 eggs
1 teaspoon vanilla
1½ cups flaked coconut
1 cup toffee baking bits
½ cup bittersweet chocolate chips

1. Preheat oven to 350°F. Line cookie sheets with parchment paper. Combine flour, baking powder and salt in small bowl.

2. Combine 1 cup semisweet chocolate chips and butter in medium microwavable bowl. Microwave on HIGH 1 minute; stir. Microwave at additional 30-second intervals until mixture is melted and smooth, stirring after each interval.

3. Beat brown sugar, eggs and vanilla in large bowl with electric mixer at medium speed until creamy. Beat in chocolate mixture until well blended. Gradually add flour mixture at low speed, beating just until blended. Stir in coconut, toffee bits and remaining 1 cup semisweet chocolate chips. Drop dough by heaping ⅓ cupfuls 3 inches apart onto prepared cookie sheets. Flatten with spatula into 3½-inch circles.

4. Bake 15 to 17 minutes or until edges are firm to the touch. Cool on cookie sheets 2 minutes; slide parchment paper and cookies onto wire racks to cool completely.

5. For chocolate drizzle, place bittersweet chocolate chips in small microwavable bowl. Microwave on HIGH 30 seconds; stir. Microwave at additional 30-second intervals until melted and smooth, stirring after each interval. Drizzle over cookies with fork. Let stand until set.

Chocolate Cookie Pops

2 cups all-purpose flour

½ cup unsweetened cocoa powder

½ teaspoon baking powder

½ teaspoon salt

1 cup (2 sticks) unsalted butter, softened

1 cup granulated sugar, plus additional for flattening cookies

½ cup packed brown sugar

1 egg

1 teaspoon vanilla

½ cup semisweet chocolate chips

1 teaspoon shortening, divided

½ cup white chocolate chips or chopped white chocolate candy bar

Sprinkles and decors

1. Preheat oven to 350°F. Combine flour, cocoa, baking powder and salt in small bowl.

2. Beat butter, 1 cup granulated sugar and brown sugar in large bowl with electric mixer at medium-high speed until light and fluffy. Beat in egg and vanilla until well blended. Gradually add flour mixture at low speed, beating just until blended.

3. Drop dough by scant ¼ cupfuls (2 ounces each) onto ungreased or parchment-lined cookie sheets, spacing 3 inches apart. Dip bottom of glass in granulated sugar; press dough to flatten cookies until 2 inches in diameter. Insert popsicle stick 1½ inches into each cookie.

4. Bake 14 to 16 minutes or until cookies are set. Cool on cookie sheets 10 minutes. If necessary, trim uneven crispy edges from cookies with sharp knife. Remove to wire racks to cool completely.

5. Combine semisweet chocolate chips and ½ teaspoon shortening in small microwavable bowl. Microwave on HIGH 30 seconds; stir. Continue microwaving at 10-second intervals until melted and smooth. Repeat with white chocolate chips and remaining ½ teaspoon shortening. Place glazes in separate small resealable food storage bags with small corners cut off. Pipe in spiral shape on cookies; immediately sprinkle with decors. Let stand until set.

TIP: Instead of using wooden pop sticks, try colorful paper straws. Bake cookies as directed without sticks and immediately remove to wire racks. Carefully insert a straw into each hot cookie all the way to the top. Cool completely.

Holiday Triple Chocolate Yule Logs

1¾ cups all-purpose flour
¾ cup powdered sugar
¼ cup unsweetened cocoa powder
¼ teaspoon salt

1 cup (2 sticks) unsalted butter, softened
1 teaspoon vanilla
1 cup white chocolate chips
Chocolate sprinkles

1. Combine flour, powdered sugar, cocoa and salt in medium bowl. Beat butter and vanilla in large bowl with electric mixer at medium-high speed until fluffy. Gradually beat in flour mixture until well blended. Wrap dough in plastic wrap; refrigerate 30 minutes or until firm.

2. Preheat oven to 350°F. Shape dough into 2-inch logs about ½ inch thick. Place 2 inches apart on ungreased cookie sheets.

3. Bake 12 minutes or until set. Cool on cookie sheets 2 minutes. Remove to wire racks; cool completely.

4. Place white chocolate chips in small microwavable bowl. Microwave on HIGH 30 seconds. Microwave at 30-second intervals, stirring until smooth. Place chocolate sprinkles in another small bowl. Dip both ends of cooled cookies first into melted white chocolate and then into chocolate sprinkles. Place on wire racks. Let stand 25 minutes to set.

Chocolate Peppermint Kisses

2 egg whites

¼ teaspoon salt

¾ cup granulated sugar

½ cup mini semisweet chocolate chips

5 hard peppermint candies, finely crushed*

½ teaspoon vanilla

2 to 3 drops red food coloring

Chocolate, red or holiday sprinkles

To crush, place unwrapped candy in a large resealable food storage bag. Loosely seal the bag, leaving an opening for air to escape. Crush with a rolling pin, meat mallet or heavy skillet.

1. Preheat oven to 200°F. Line cookie sheets with parchment paper.

2. Beat egg whites and salt in medium bowl with electric mixer at high speed until soft peaks form. Gradually add sugar, beating until stiff peaks form.

3. Fold in chocolate chips, peppermint candies, vanilla and food coloring. Drop by teaspoonfuls onto prepared cookie sheets. Top each cookie with sprinkles.

4. Turn off oven. Place cookie sheets in oven; let stand 45 minutes or until dry and crisp. (Do not open oven.) Kisses may be left overnight to dry. Store in airtight container.

TIP: For best volume, let egg whites stand at room temperature for 30 minutes before beating. Also, egg whites must be completely free of egg yolk. The smallest trace of yolk, fat or water can prevent the whites from reaching maximum volume.

Chocolate-Frosted Marshmallow Cookies

COOKIES

- ½ cup (1 stick) unsalted butter
- 2 ounces unsweetened chocolate, chopped
- 1 egg
- 1 cup packed brown sugar
- 2 teaspoons vanilla, divided
- ½ teaspoon baking soda
- ¼ teaspoon salt
- 1½ cups all-purpose flour
- ½ cup milk

TOPPING

- 1 package (16 ounces) large marshmallows, halved crosswise
- 1½ ounces unsweetened chocolate, chopped
- ¼ cup (½ stick) unsalted butter
- 1½ cups powdered sugar
- 1 egg white*

Use clean, uncracked egg.

1. Preheat oven to 350°F. Lightly grease cookie sheets or line with parchment paper.

2. Melt ½ cup butter and 2 ounces chocolate in small heavy saucepan over low heat; stir to blend. Remove from heat; cool. Beat egg, brown sugar, 1 teaspoon vanilla, baking soda and salt in large bowl with electric mixer at medium speed until light and fluffy. Beat in chocolate mixture and flour until smooth. Beat in milk at low speed until light. Drop dough by teaspoonfuls 2 inches apart onto prepared cookie sheets.

3. Bake 10 minutes or until set. Immediately place a halved marshmallow, cut side down, on each baked cookie. Bake 1 minute or just until marshmallow is warm enough to stick to cookie. Remove to wire racks; cool completely.

4. For frosting, melt 1½ ounces chocolate and ¼ cup butter in small heavy saucepan over low heat, stirring until smooth. Beat in powdered sugar. Beat in egg white and remaining 1 teaspoon vanilla, adding a little water, if necessary, to make a smooth, slightly soft frosting. Spoon frosting over cookies to cover marshmallows.

Chocolate Coconut Pecan Crisps

MAKES ABOUT 6 DOZEN COOKIES

1½ cups all-purpose flour

1 cup chopped pecans

⅓ cup unsweetened cocoa powder

½ teaspoon baking soda

½ teaspoon salt

1 cup packed brown sugar

½ cup (1 stick) unsalted butter, softened

1 egg

1 teaspoon vanilla

1 cup flaked coconut

1. Combine flour, pecans, cocoa, baking soda and salt in small bowl. Beat brown sugar and butter in large bowl with electric mixer at medium speed until light and fluffy. Beat in egg and vanilla. Gradually add flour mixture at low speed, beating until stiff dough forms.

2. Sprinkle coconut on work surface. Divide dough into four pieces. Shape each piece into log about 1½ inches in diameter; roll in coconut until thickly coated. Wrap in plastic wrap; refrigerate until firm, at least 1 hour or up to 2 weeks. (For longer storage, freeze up to 6 weeks.)

3. Preheat oven to 350°F. Cut dough into ⅛-inch-thick slices. Place 2 inches apart on ungreased cookie sheets.

4. Bake 10 to 11 minutes or just until firm. Cool on cookie sheets 1 minute. Remove to wire racks; cool completely.

Cocoa-Oatmeal Cookies

MAKES 4 DOZEN COOKIES

½ cup (1 stick) unsalted butter, softened

½ cup granulated sugar

½ cup packed brown sugar

1 egg

½ teaspoon vanilla

¾ cup all-purpose flour

¼ cup unsweetened cocoa powder

½ teaspoon baking powder

½ teaspoon salt

1½ cups quick or old-fashioned oats

1 cup milk chocolate chips

½ cup chopped macadamia nuts, toasted*

To toast macadamias, place in single layer on ungreased baking sheet. Bake in preheated 350°F oven 8 to 10 minutes or until lightly browned, stirring occasionally. Cool before using.

1. Preheat oven to 350°F. Line cookie sheets with parchment paper.

2. Beat butter in medium bowl with electric mixer at medium speed until light and fluffy. Add granulated sugar and brown sugar; beat until well blended. Add egg and vanilla; beat just until combined. Add flour, cocoa, baking powder and salt; beat at low speed just until blended (dough will be sticky and stiff). Stir in oats, chocolate chips and nuts.

3. Shape dough into 1-inch balls. Place 2 inches apart on prepared cookie sheets. Slightly flatten each ball with back of spoon.

4. Bake 7 to 9 minutes or until firm around edges. Cool on cookie sheets 5 minutes. Remove to wire racks; cool completely.

Deep Dark Chocolate Drops

MAKES ABOUT 3 DOZEN COOKIES

1¼ cups all-purpose flour
¼ cup unsweetened cocoa powder
½ teaspoon salt
½ teaspoon baking soda
1½ cups semisweet chocolate chips, divided

½ cup (1 stick) unsalted butter, softened
½ cup granulated sugar
¼ cup packed brown sugar
1 egg
2 tablespoons milk
1 teaspoon vanilla

1. Preheat oven to 350°F. Lightly grease cookie sheets or line with parchment paper. Combine flour, cocoa, salt and baking soda in medium bowl.

2. Place ½ cup chocolate chips in small microwavable bowl. Microwave on HIGH 1 minute; stir. Microwave at additional 30-second intervals until chips are melted and smooth. Let cool slightly.

3. Beat butter, granulated sugar and brown sugar in large bowl with electric mixer at medium-high until light and fluffy. Add egg, milk, vanilla and melted chocolate; beat until well blended. Gradually add flour mixture at low speed, beating just until blended. Stir in remaining 1 cup chocolate chips. Drop dough by tablespoons at least 2 inches apart onto prepared cookie sheets.

4. Bake 10 to 11 minutes or until set and no longer shiny. Cool on cookie sheets 2 minutes. Remove to wire racks; cool completely.

Nutty Chocolate Coconut Cookies

2 ounces unsweetened chocolate, chopped
1 cup packed brown sugar
½ cup (1 stick) unsalted butter, softened
1 egg
1¼ cups all-purpose flour
¼ teaspoon baking powder
¼ teaspoon salt
⅛ teaspoon baking soda
2 cups chopped pecans or walnuts
½ cup flaked coconut

1. Preheat oven to 350°F. Lightly grease cookie sheets or line with parchment paper.

2. Melt chocolate in top of double boiler over hot, not boiling, water. Remove from heat; cool. Beat brown sugar and butter in large bowl with electric mixer at medium-high speed 3 minutes or light and fluffy. Add egg and melted chocolate; beat until well blended. Combine flour, baking powder, salt and baking soda in small bowl. Stir into butter mixture until blended. Stir in pecans and coconut. Drop dough by teaspoonfuls 2 inches apart onto prepared cookie sheets.

3. Bake 10 to 12 minutes or until firm. Cool on cookie sheets 2 minutes. Remove to wire racks; cool completely.

Chocolate Peppermint Crackle Cookies

MAKES 2 DOZEN COOKIES

9 to 10 peppermint hard candies*

1⅓ cups all-purpose flour

¾ cup unsweetened cocoa powder

1 teaspoon instant espresso powder

½ teaspoon baking soda

¼ teaspoon baking powder

¼ teaspoon salt

¾ cup (1½ sticks) unsalted butter, softened

¾ cup packed brown sugar

¼ cup granulated sugar

1 egg

2 ounces bittersweet chocolate, finely chopped

*Or substitute candy canes, ground to measure ¼ cup.

1. Preheat oven to 350°F. Line cookie sheets with parchment paper. Place peppermint candies in food processor; pulse until fine powder forms. Place in medium bowl. Add flour, cocoa, espresso powder, baking soda, baking powder and salt.

2. Beat butter, brown sugar and granulated sugar in large bowl with electric mixer at medium-high speed 3 minutes or until light and fluffy. Add egg; beat until well blended. With mixer running at low speed, gradually add flour mixture. Stir in chocolate.

3. For each cookie, roll 2 tablespoonfuls of dough into a ball. Place balls 2 inches apart on prepared cookie sheets.

4. Bake 11 to 13 minutes or until tops are cracked, edges are set and centers are still soft. Cool on cookie sheets 10 minutes. Remove to wire racks; cool completely.

Extra-Chocolatey Brownie Cookies

2 cups all-purpose flour

½ cup unsweetened Dutch process cocoa powder

1 teaspoon baking soda

¾ teaspoon salt

1 cup (2 sticks) unsalted butter, softened

1 cup packed brown sugar

½ cup granulated sugar

2 eggs

2 teaspoons vanilla

1 package (11½ ounces) semisweet chocolate chunks

2 cups coarsely chopped walnuts or pecans

1. Preheat oven to 350°F. Combine flour, cocoa, baking soda and salt in medium bowl until well blended.

2. Beat butter, brown sugar and granulated sugar in large bowl with electric mixer at medium speed until light and fluffy. Add eggs and vanilla; beat until well blended. Gradually add flour mixture at low speed, beating just until blended. Stir in chocolate chunks and walnuts.

3. Drop dough by heaping tablespoonfuls 2 inches apart onto ungreased cookie sheets; flatten slightly.

4. Bake 8 to 10 minutes or until set. Cool on cookie sheets 2 minutes. Remove to wire racks; cool completely.

Chocolate Cherry Cookies

½ cup (1 stick) unsalted butter, softened
¾ cup granulated sugar
1 egg
1 teaspoon vanilla
½ teaspoon salt

1½ cups all-purpose flour
½ cup unsweetened cocoa powder
30 stemmed maraschino cherries, and well drained
¼ cup white chocolate chips
1 teaspoon canola oil

1. Beat butter and granulated sugar in large bowl with electric mixer at medium speed until light and fluffy. Add egg, vanilla and salt; beat until well blended. Add flour and cocoa; beat at low speed just until blended. Shape dough into a ball; wrap in plastic wrap and refrigerate 1 hour or until firm.

2. Preheat oven to 350°F. Line cookie sheet with parchment paper. Shape dough into 1-inch balls; place 1 inch apart on prepared cookie sheet. Make indentation in each ball with thumb or fingertip; place cherry into each indentation.

3. Bake 8 minutes or just until set. Cool completely on cookie sheet.

4. For glaze, place white chocolate chips and oil in small microwavable bowl. Microwave on HIGH 30 seconds; stir. Microwave at 30-second intervals until chocolate is melted and mixture is smooth. Drizzle over cookies on cookie sheet; let stand until set.

TIP: To prevent dough from cracking, make the indentations immediately after rolling each ball of dough.

VARIATION: Instead of the white chocolate glaze, drizzle with dark chocolate instead. Melt 4 ounces of bittersweet chocolate and drizzle over cooled cookies. Let stand until set.

CLASSIC BUTTER COOKIES

Refrigerator Cookies

MAKES ABOUT 4 DOZEN COOKIES

1¾ cups all-purpose flour
¼ teaspoon baking soda
¼ teaspoon salt
½ cup granulated sugar
¼ cup light corn syrup

¼ cup (½ stick) unsalted butter, softened
1 egg
1 teaspoon vanilla
Nonpareils and decorating sugars (optional)

1. Combine flour, baking soda and salt in medium bowl. Beat sugar, corn syrup and butter in large bowl with electric mixer at medium speed until well blended. Add egg and vanilla; mix well. Gradually add flour mixture at low speed, beating just until blended.

2. Shape dough into two rolls 1½ inches in diameter. Wrap in plastic wrap. Freeze 1 hour.

3. Preheat oven to 350°F. Line cookie sheets with parchment paper. Cut dough into ¼-inch-thick slices; place 1 inch apart on prepared cookie sheets. Sprinkle with decors, if desired.

4. Bake 8 to 10 minutes or until edges are lightly brown. Remove to wire racks; cool completely.

VARIATIONS: Add 2 tablespoons unsweetened cocoa powder to dough for chocolate cookies. For sugar-rimmed cookies, roll logs in colored sugar before slicing.

Benne Wafers

¾ cup all-purpose flour
¼ teaspoon salt
¼ teaspoon baking powder
½ cup sesame seeds

½ cup (1 stick) unsalted butter, softened
½ cup packed light brown sugar
1 egg
½ teaspoon vanilla

1. Preheat oven to 350°F. Line two cookie sheets with parchment paper. Combine flour, salt and baking powder in small bowl.

2. Spread sesame seeds on small rimmed baking sheet. Toast 5 minutes or until lightly browned. Transfer seeds to bowl to cool.

3. Beat butter and brown sugar in medium bowl with electric mixer at high speed until light and fluffy. Beat in egg and vanilla. Gradually beat in flour mixture. Add sesame seeds; beat until well blended.

4. Drop dough by rounded teaspoonfuls 2 inches apart onto prepared cookie sheets. Flatten slightly with fork.

5. Bake 9 to 10 minutes or until lightly browned. Cool on cookie sheets 5 minutes. Remove to wire racks; cool completely.

Mexican Wedding Cookies

MAKES ABOUT 4 DOZEN COOKIES

1 cup pecan pieces or halves
1 cup (2 sticks) unsalted butter, softened
2 cups powdered sugar, divided

2 teaspoons vanilla
½ teaspoon salt
2 cups all-purpose flour

1. Place pecans in food processor; pulse until pecans are ground but not pasty.

2. Beat butter and ½ cup powdered sugar in large bowl with electric mixer at medium speed until light and fluffy. Add vanilla and salt; beat until well blended. Gradually add flour at low speed, beating just until blended. Stir in ground nuts. Shape dough into a ball; wrap in plastic wrap. Refrigerate 1 hour or until firm.

3. Preheat oven to 350°F. Shape dough into 1-inch balls. Place 1 inch apart on ungreased cookie sheets.

4. Bake 12 to 15 minutes or until golden brown. Cool on cookie sheets 2 minutes.

5. Meanwhile, place 1 cup powdered sugar in 13X9-inch baking dish. Transfer hot cookies to powdered sugar. Roll cookies in powdered sugar, coating well. Let cookies cool in sugar in dish.

6. Sift remaining ½ cup powdered sugar over cookies just before serving.

Browned Butter Spritz Cookies

1½ cups (3 sticks) unsalted butter
2½ cups all-purpose flour
¼ cup cake flour
¼ teaspoon salt
½ cup granulated sugar

¼ cup powdered sugar
1 egg yolk
1 teaspoon vanilla
⅛ teaspoon almond extract
Decorating gels, sugars, sprinkles and decors (optional)

1. Melt butter in medium heavy saucepan over medium heat; cook until butter is light amber and smells nutty, swirling pan frequently. Transfer butter to large bowl. Cover and refrigerate 2 hours or until solid.

2. Preheat oven to 350°F. Let browned butter stand at room temperature 15 minutes. Combine all-purpose flour, cake flour and salt in small bowl.

3. Beat browned butter, granulated sugar and powdered sugar in large bowl with electric mixer at medium speed until light and fluffy. Add egg yolk, vanilla and almond extract; beat until well blended. Gradually add flour mixture at low speed, beating just until blended.

4. Fit cookie press with desired plate (or change plates for different shapes after first batch). Fill press with dough; press dough 1 inch apart onto ungreased cookie sheets. Decorate with sugar, sprinkles, decors or gels, if desired.

5. Bake 10 minutes or until lightly browned. Cool on cookie sheets 5 minutes. Remove to wire racks; cool completely.

Candy-Studded Wreaths

MAKES ABOUT 2 DOZEN COOKIES

1 cup (2 sticks) unsalted butter, softened
½ cup powdered sugar
2 tablespoons packed brown sugar
¼ teaspoon salt
1 egg
1 teaspoon vanilla
2 cups all-purpose flour
4 to 5 drops green food coloring
Mini red and green candy-coated chocolate pieces

1. Beat butter, powdered sugar, brown sugar and salt in large bowl with electric mixer at medium speed 2 minutes or until light and fluffy. Add egg and vanilla; beat until well blended.

2. Add flour, ½ cup at a time, beating well after each addition. Divide dough in half; set one half aside. Add green color to remaining dough; beat until blended. Shape both doughs into balls; wrap in plastic wrap and chill 1 hour.

3. Preheat oven to 300°F. Shape green dough into 28 (5-inch) ropes. Repeat with plain dough. For each wreath, twist 1 green and 1 plain rope together, pressing ends together. Place on ungreased cookie sheets. Press candies onto wreaths.

4. Bake 15 to 18 minutes or until lightly browned. Cool on cookie sheets 5 minutes. Remove to wire racks; cool completely.

Pistachio Lemon Shortbread Cookies

1 cup (2 sticks) unsalted butter, softened
½ cup packed brown sugar
¼ cup powdered sugar
Grated peel of 1 lemon
½ teaspoon salt
½ teaspoon vanilla

2 cups all-purpose flour
1¼ cups coarsely chopped pistachios, toasted*
½ cup white chocolate chips

*To toast pistachios, place in single layer on ungreased baking sheet. Bake in preheated 350°F oven 8 to 10 minutes or until lightly browned, stirring occasionally. Cool before using.

1. Preheat oven to 300°F. Line cookie sheets with parchment paper or leave ungreased.

2. Beat butter, brown sugar and powdered sugar in large bowl with electric mixer at medium-high speed 5 minutes or until light and fluffy. Add lemon peel, salt and vanilla; mix well. With mixer running on low speed, gradually add flour. Add pistachios and white chocolate chips; mix just until blended.

3. Shape dough by tablespoons into 1-inch balls; place on cookie sheets and flatten slightly with fingers.

4. Bake 15 minutes or until lightly browned around edges. Cool on cookie sheets 5 minutes. Remove to wire racks; cool completely.

Spumone Bars

¾ cup (1½ sticks) unsalted butter, softened

⅔ cup granulated sugar

3 egg yolks

1 teaspoon vanilla

¼ teaspoon baking powder

¼ teaspoon salt

2 cups all-purpose flour

12 maraschino cherries, well drained and chopped

¼ cup chopped walnuts

¼ cup mint-flavored or plain semisweet chocolate chips, melted and cooled slightly

2 teaspoons water, divided

1. Preheat oven to 350°F.

2. Beat butter and sugar in large bowl with electric mixer at medium-high speed 3 minutes or until blended. Add egg yolks, vanilla, baking powder and salt; beat until light and fluffy. Stir in flour to make a stiff dough. Divide dough into 3 equal parts; place each part in separate small bowl. Add cherries and walnuts to one part, mixing well. Add melted chocolate and 1 teaspoon water to second part, mixing well. Stir remaining 1 teaspoon water into third part. (If doughs are soft, refrigerate 10 minutes.)

3. Divide each color dough into 4 equal parts. Shape each part into 6-inch rope by rolling on lightly floured surface. Place one rope of each color side by side on ungreased cookie sheet. Flatten ropes so they attach together making 1 strip of 3 colors. With rolling pin, roll strip directly on cookie sheet until it measures 12X3 inches. With sharp knife, score strip crosswise at 1-inch intervals. Repeat with remaining ropes to make total of 4 tri-colored strips of dough.

4. Bake 12 to 13 minutes or until set but not completely browned; remove from oven. While cookies are still warm, trim lengthwise edges to make them even and cut into individual cookies along score marks. (Cookies will bake together but are easy to cut apart while still warm.) Cool completely on cookie sheets.

Black & White Hearts

1 cup (2 sticks) unsalted butter, softened
¾ cup granulated sugar
3 ounces cream cheese, softened
1 egg
1½ teaspoons vanilla
3 cups all-purpose flour
½ teaspoon salt
1 cup semisweet chocolate chips
2 tablespoons shortening

1. Beat butter, sugar, cream cheese, egg and vanilla in large bowl with electric mixer at medium speed until light and fluffy. Add flour and salt; beat until well blended. Divide dough in half; wrap each half in plastic wrap. Refrigerate 2 hours or until firm.

2. Preheat oven to 375°F. Roll dough to ⅛-inch thickness on lightly floured surface. Cut dough with lightly floured 2-inch heart-shaped cookie cutter. Place cutouts 1 inch apart on ungreased cookie sheets.

3. Bake 7 to 10 minutes or until edges are lightly browned. Immediately remove to wire racks; cool completely.

4. Melt chocolate chips and shortening in small saucepan over low heat, stirring constantly until smooth. Dip half of each heart into melted chocolate; scrape bottom of cookie along edge of saucepan to remove excess chocolate. Refrigerate on cookie sheets or trays lined with waxed paper until chocolate is set.

Peppermint Wafers

2 cups all-purpose flour

½ cup plus 1 tablespoon unsweetened cocoa powder, sifted, divided

1 teaspoon baking powder

½ teaspoon salt

¾ cup (1½ sticks) unsalted butter, softened

1 cup granulated sugar

1 egg

4 teaspoons vanilla, divided

1 to 1½ teaspoons peppermint extract

3 cups powdered sugar

¼ cup hot water or milk (not boiling)

1. Combine flour, ½ cup cocoa, baking powder and salt in small bowl. Beat butter and granulated sugar in large bowl with electric mixer at medium speed 1 minute or until creamy. Add egg, 1 teaspoon vanilla and peppermint extract; beat until well blended. Gradually stir in flour mixture on low speed just until blended.

2. Shape dough into 12X2-inch log on lightly floured work surface. Wrap tightly in waxed paper, then wrap in plastic wrap. Freeze 2 hours or until firm.

3. Preheat oven to 350°F. Grease cookie sheets or line with parchment paper. Cut dough into ⅛-inch slices. Place slices 1 inch apart on prepared cookie sheets.

4. Bake 9 minutes or until puffed and firm to the touch. Cool on cookie sheets 2 minutes. Remove to wire racks; cool completely.

5. For icing, combine powdered sugar, hot water and remaining 3 teaspoons vanilla in medium bowl; stir until smooth. Add additional water, ½ teaspoon at a time, if necessary, until desired consistency is reached. Divide icing in half. Add remaining 1 tablespoon cocoa to one bowl; stir until well blended. Cover until ready to use.

6. Frost cooled cookies with vanilla icing; let stand until set. Drizzle cookies with chocolate icing; let stand until set.

Ginger Sugar Cookies

2 cups all-purpose flour
2 teaspoons ground ginger
¼ teaspoon salt
⅛ teaspoon ground white pepper

¾ cup (1½ sticks) unsalted butter, softened
¾ cup granulated sugar
1 egg yolk
Chopped crystallized ginger (optional)

1. Preheat oven to 350°F. Combine flour, ginger, salt and pepper in medium bowl.

2. Beat butter in large bowl with electric mixer at medium speed until creamy. Add sugar; beat until light and fluffy. Add egg yolk; beat until blended. Gradually add flour mixture at low speed, beating just until blended.

3. Divide dough in half. Cover half in plastic wrap and chill. Roll second half of dough between two sheets of plastic wrap to ¼-inch thickness. Cut out decorative shapes with cookie cutters. Place on ungreased cookie sheets. Press crystallized ginger into cutouts, if desired. Repeat with remaining dough.

4. Bake 13 minutes or until lightly browned on edges. Cool on cookie sheets 2 minutes. Remove to wire racks; cool completely.

Easy Holiday Shortbread Cookies

1 cup (2 sticks) unsalted butter, softened
½ cup powdered sugar
2 tablespoons packed brown sugar

¼ teaspoon salt
2 cups all-purpose flour
Red, white and green decorating sugars (optional)

1. Beat butter, powdered sugar, brown sugar and salt in large bowl with electric mixer at medium speed 2 minutes or until light and fluffy. Add flour, ½ cup at a time, beating well after each addition. Shape dough into 14-inch-long square log. Cut log into thirds. Roll each third in red, white and green decorating sugars, if desired. Wrap logs tightly in plastic wrap; refrigerate 1 hour.

2. Preheat oven to 300°F. Cut logs into ½-inch-thick slices; place on ungreased cookie sheets.

3. Bake 20 to 25 minutes or until lightly browned. Cool on cookie sheets 5 minutes. Remove to wire racks; cool completely.

NOTE: This dough can be stored in the refrigerator for up to 2 days or in the freezer for up to 1 month. Thaw frozen dough in the refrigerator overnight before slicing and baking.

Buttery Almond Cookies

1¼ cups all-purpose flour

½ teaspoon baking powder

¼ teaspoon salt

10 tablespoons unsalted butter, softened

¾ cup granulated sugar

1 egg

1 teaspoon vanilla

¾ cup slivered almonds, finely chopped

½ cup slivered almonds (optional)

1. Preheat oven to 350°F. Grease cookie sheets or line with parchment paper. Combine flour, baking powder and salt in small bowl.

2. Beat butter in large bowl with electric mixer at medium speed until smooth. Gradually beat in sugar until blended. Increase speed to high; beat until light and fluffy. Beat in egg and vanilla. Gradually add flour mixture on low speed, beating just until blended. Stir in chopped almonds.

3. Drop rounded teaspoonfuls of dough 2 inches apart on prepared cookie sheets. Press several slivered almonds into each cookie, if desired.

4. Bake 12 minutes or until edges are golden brown. Cool on cookie sheets 5 minutes. Remove to wire racks; cool completely.

Butter Pecan Crisps

2½ cups sifted all-purpose flour
1 teaspoon baking soda
½ teaspoon salt
1 cup (2 sticks) unsalted butter, softened
¾ cup granulated sugar
¾ cup packed brown sugar

2 eggs
1 teaspoon vanilla
1½ cups finely ground pecans
30 pecan halves
4 ounces semisweet chocolate
1 tablespoon shortening

1. Preheat oven to 375°F. Line cookie sheets with parchment paper. Combine flour, baking soda and salt in small bowl.

2. Beat butter, granulated sugar and brown sugar in large bowl with electric mixer at medium speed until light and fluffy. Add eggs, one at a time, beating well after each addition. Beat in vanilla, then ground pecans. Gradually add flour mixture at low speed, beating just until blended.

3. Spoon dough into large pastry bag fitted with ⅜-inch round tip; fill bag halfway. Shake down dough to remove air bubbles. Hold bag perpendicular to, and about ½ inch above, prepared cookie sheets. Pipe dough into 1¼-inch balls, spacing 3 inches apart. Cut each pecan half lengthwise into 2 slivers. Press 1 sliver in center of each dough ball.

4. Bake 10 minutes or until lightly browned. Cool on cookie sheets 5 minutes. Remove to wire racks; cool completely.

5. Melt chocolate and shortening in small heavy saucepan over low heat, stirring constantly until melted and smooth. Drizzle over cookies; let stand until set.

Pistachio Crescent Cookies

2 cups all-purpose flour

2 cups finely chopped salted pistachios, divided

¼ teaspoon salt

1¼ cups (2½ sticks) unsalted butter, softened, divided

¾ cup powdered sugar

½ cup mini chocolate chips

⅔ cup semisweet chocolate chips

1. Line cookie sheets with parchment paper. Combine flour, 1½ cups pistachios and salt in medium bowl; mix well.

2. Beat 1 cup butter and powdered sugar in large bowl with electric mixer until fluffy. Gradually add flour mixture at low speed, beating just until blended. Stir in mini chocolate chips just until blended. Roll 1½ teaspoons dough into 2½-inch ropes; bend into crescent shapes. Arrange 1 inch apart on prepared cookie sheets. Chill 30 minutes.

3. Preheat oven to 300°F. Bake cookies 10 minutes or until firm and lightly browned. Cool on cookie sheets 1 minute. Remove to wire racks; cool completely.

4. For glaze, combine ⅔ cup chocolate chips and remaining ¼ cup butter in microwavable bowl. Microwave on LOW (30%) 1 minute. Stir and repeat until chocolate is melted and mixture is smooth. Place cookies on wire rack over waxed paper. Place remaining ½ cup pistachios in small bowl. Dip one end of each cookie in chocolate, then in nuts. Let stand 30 minutes or until chocolate is set.

Danish Cookie Rings (Vanillekranser)

MAKES ABOUT 5 DOZEN COOKIES

½ cup blanched almonds

2 cups all-purpose flour

¾ cup granulated sugar

¼ teaspoon baking powder

¼ teaspoon salt

1 cup (2 sticks) unsalted butter, cut into small pieces

1 egg

1 tablespoon milk

1 tablespoon vanilla

15 candied red cherries

15 candied green cherries

1. Pulse almonds in food processor until finely ground but not pasty. Add flour, sugar, baking powder and salt; pulse until blended. Add butter; pulse until mixture is crumbly. Transfer to large bowl.

2. Beat egg, milk and vanilla in small bowl until well blended. Add egg mixture to flour mixture; stir until soft dough forms.

3. Grease cookie sheets or line with parchment paper. Spoon dough into pastry bag fitted with medium star tip. Pipe 3-inch rings 2 inches apart on prepared cookie sheets. Refrigerate 15 minutes or until firm.

4. Preheat oven to 375°F. Cut red cherries into quarters. Cut green cherries into halves; cut each half into 4 slivers. Press red cherry quarter onto each ring where ends meet. Place green cherry sliver on either side of red cherry to form leaves.

5. Bake 8 to 10 minutes or until golden. Cool on cookie sheets 2 minutes. Remove to wire racks; cool completely.

Frosted Butter Cookies

COOKIES

- 3 cups all-purpose flour
- 1 teaspoon baking powder
- ½ teaspoon salt
- 1½ cups (3 sticks) unsalted butter, softened
- ¾ cup granulated sugar
- 3 egg yolks
- 2 tablespoons orange juice
- 1 teaspoon vanilla

ROYAL ICING

- ¼ cup plus 2 tablespoons water
- ¼ cup meringue powder*
- 1 box (16 ounces) powdered sugar, sifted
- Decorating sugars and decors (optional)

Meringue powder is available where cake decorating supplies are sold.

1. Combine flour, baking powder and salt in medium bowl. Beat butter and granulated sugar in large bowl with electric mixer at medium-high speed until creamy. Add egg yolks, orange juice and vanilla; beat until blended. Gradually add flour mixture at low speed, beating just until blended. Shape dough into two discs; wrap in plastic wrap. Refrigerate 2 to 3 hours or until firm.

2. Preheat oven to 350°F. Roll out dough, half at a time, to ¼-inch thickness on well-floured surface. Cut dough with cookie cutters. Place 1 inch apart on ungreased cookie sheets. Bake 6 to 10 minutes or until edges are lightly browned. Cool on cookie sheets 2 minutes. Remove to wire racks; cool completely.

3. For icing, beat water and meringue powder in medium bowl with electric mixer at low speed until well blended. Beat at medium-high speed about 5 minutes or until stiff peaks form.

4. Beat in powdered sugar at low speed until well blended. Beat at high speed until icing is very stiff. Cover icing with damp cloth to prevent it from drying out. Tint icing desired colors; pipe or spread on cookies. Decorate with sugars, if desired.

VARIATION: Use buttercream icing instead of royal icing. Beat 4 cups powdered sugar, ½ cup (1 stick) softened butter, 3 tablespoons milk and 2 teaspoons vanilla in large bowl with electric mixer at low speed until blended. Beat at medium-high speed until light and fluffy. Tint desired colors and pipe onto cookies.

FESTIVE FRUIT & SPICE COOKIES

Holiday Fruit Drops

MAKES ABOUT 8 DOZEN COOKIES

¾ cup packed brown sugar

½ cup (1 stick) unsalted butter, softened

1 egg

1¼ cups all-purpose flour

1 teaspoon vanilla

½ teaspoon baking soda

½ teaspoon ground cinnamon

¼ teaspoon salt

1 cup (8 ounces) diced candied pineapple

1 cup (8 ounces) whole red and green candied cherries*

1 cup (8 ounces) chopped pitted dates

1 cup semisweet chocolate chips

½ cup whole hazelnuts*

½ cup pecan halves*

½ cup coarsely chopped walnuts

The cherries, hazelnuts and pecan halves are not chopped, but left whole.

1. Preheat oven to 325°F. Grease cookie sheets or line with parchment paper.

2. Beat brown sugar and butter in large bowl with electric mixer until creamy. Beat in egg until light and fluffy. Add flour, vanilla, baking soda, cinnamon and salt; beat just until blended. Stir in pineapple, cherries, dates, chocolate chips, hazelnuts, pecans and walnuts. Drop dough by rounded teaspoonfuls 2 inches apart onto prepared cookie sheets.

3. Bake 15 to 20 minutes or until firm and lightly browned around edges. Cool on cookie sheets 2 minutes. Remove to wire racks; cool completely.

Gingery Oat & Molasses Cookies

MAKES ABOUT 4 DOZEN COOKIES

1 cup all-purpose flour

¾ cup whole wheat flour

½ cup old-fashioned oats

1½ teaspoons baking powder

1½ teaspoons ground ginger

1 teaspoon baking soda

½ teaspoon ground cinnamon

¼ teaspoon salt

¾ cup granulated sugar

½ cup (1 stick) unsalted butter, softened

1 egg

¼ cup molasses

¼ teaspoon vanilla

1 cup chopped crystallized ginger

½ cup chopped walnuts

1. Combine all-purpose flour, whole wheat flour, oats, baking powder, ground ginger, baking soda, cinnamon and salt in medium bowl.

2. Beat sugar and butter in large bowl with electric mixer at high speed until light and fluffy. Beat in egg, molasses and vanilla. Gradually add flour mixture at low speed, beating just until blended. Stir in crystallized ginger and walnuts.

3. Shape dough into two 8- to 10-inch logs. Wrap in plastic wrap; refrigerate 1 to 3 hours.

4. Preheat oven to 350°F. Grease cookie sheets or line with parchment paper. Cut logs into ⅓-inch slices; place 1½ inches apart on prepared cookie sheets.

5. Bake 12 to 14 minutes or until set. Cool on cookie sheets 5 minutes. Remove to wire racks; cool completely.

Date-Nut Cookies

MAKES 2 DOZEN COOKIES

1 cup chopped dates
½ cup water
1¾ cups all-purpose flour
½ teaspoon baking powder
¼ teaspoon salt

½ cup (1 stick) unsalted butter, softened
½ cup packed dark brown sugar
1 egg
2 teaspoons rum extract
½ cup walnut pieces, chopped

1. Soak dates in water in small bowl at least 30 minutes or up to 2 hours.

2. Preheat oven to 350°F. Grease cookie sheets or line with parchment paper. Combine flour, baking powder and salt in medium bowl.

3. Beat butter in large bowl with electric mixer at medium speed until smooth. Gradually beat in brown sugar; increase speed to high and beat until light and fluffy. Beat in egg and rum extract until fluffy. Gradually stir in flour mixture alternately with date mixture, mixing just until combined after each addition. Stir in walnuts until blended.

4. Drop level tablespoonfuls of dough about 1½ inches apart onto prepared cookie sheets. Bake 14 minutes or until just set. Cool on cookie sheets 2 minutes. Remove to wire racks; cool completely.

Danish Raspberry Ribbons

COOKIES
- 1 cup (2 sticks) unsalted butter, softened
- ½ cup granulated sugar
- 1 egg
- 2 tablespoons milk
- 2 teaspoons vanilla
- ½ teaspoon salt
- ¼ teaspoon almond extract
- 2⅔ cups all-purpose flour, divided
- 6 tablespoons seedless raspberry jam

GLAZE
- ½ cup powdered sugar
- 1 tablespoon milk
- 1 teaspoon vanilla

1. Beat butter and granulated sugar in large bowl with electric mixer at medium speed until light and fluffy. Beat in egg, 2 tablespoons milk, 2 teaspoons vanilla, salt and almond extract until well blended.

2. Gradually add 1½ cups flour, beating at low speed until well blended. Stir in enough remaining flour with spoon to form stiff dough. Shape dough into a disc. Wrap in plastic wrap; refrigerate until firm, at least 30 minutes or overnight.

3. Preheat oven to 375°F. Divide dough into six equal pieces. With floured hands, shape one piece at a time into ¾-inch-thick rope, about 12 inches long. (Keep remaining dough pieces wrapped in refrigerator.) Place ropes 2 inches apart on ungreased cookie sheets. Make ¼-inch-deep groove down center of each rope with handle of wooden spoon or finger.

4. Bake 12 minutes. (Ropes will flatten to ½-inch-thick strips.) Remove from oven; spoon 1 tablespoon jam into each groove. Return to oven; bake 5 to 7 minutes or until strips are light golden brown. Cool strips 15 minutes on cookie sheets.

5. For glaze, combine powdered sugar, 1 tablespoon milk and 1 teaspoon vanilla in small bowl until smooth. Drizzle over cookie strips. Let stand 5 minutes or until set. Cut cookie bars diagonally into 1-inch slices. Place cookies on wire racks; cool completely.

Lemon Raspberry Shortbread

MAKES 2 DOZEN COOKIES

1¼ cups all-purpose flour

2 tablespoons cornstarch

1½ teaspoons grated lemon peel

½ teaspoon salt

½ cup (1 stick) unsalted butter, softened

¼ cup granulated sugar

2 tablespoons plus 2 teaspoons powdered sugar

1 egg yolk

½ cup seedless raspberry jam, stirred until smooth

1. Preheat oven to 325°F. Line 8-inch square baking pan with foil or parchment paper, leaving overhang on two sides. Combine flour, cornstarch, lemon peel and salt in medium bowl.

2. Beat butter, granulated sugar and 2 tablespoons powdered sugar in large bowl with electric mixer at medium-high speed until blended. Add egg yolk; beat until light and fluffy. With mixer running on low speed, gradually add flour mixture until blended.

3. Pat dough firmly onto bottom of prepared baking pan. Bake 20 minutes. Remove from oven. Spread jam evenly over cookie base. Bake 15 minutes.

4. Lift shortbread from pan using foil; place on cutting board. While still hot, use sharp knife to cut shortbread into 24 cookies, wiping knife between cuts for clean edges. Cool completely.

Fruity Coconut Oatmeal Cookies

2 cups old-fashioned oats

1⅓ cups all-purpose flour

¾ teaspoon baking soda

½ teaspoon baking powder

½ teaspoon salt

¼ teaspoon ground cinnamon

1 cup packed brown sugar

¾ cup (1½ sticks) unsalted butter, softened

¼ cup granulated sugar

1 egg

1 tablespoon honey

1 teaspoon vanilla

½ cup finely diced dried mangoes

½ cup finely diced dried apples

½ cup finely diced dried cherries

3 cups shredded sweetened coconut, divided

1. Preheat oven to 350°F. Line cookie sheets with parchment paper. Combine oats, flour, baking soda, baking powder, salt and cinnamon in medium bowl.

2. Beat brown sugar, butter and granulated sugar in large bowl with electric mixer at medium speed until light and fluffy. Add egg, honey and vanilla; beat until well blended. Gradually add flour mixture at low speed, beating just until blended. Stir in mangoes, apples, cherries and ½ cup coconut.

3. Spread remaining 2½ cups coconut in shallow bowl. Drop dough by rounded tablespoonfuls into coconut and roll to coat; place on prepared cookie sheets.

4. Bake 15 to 17 minutes or until puffed and golden. Cool on cookie sheets 5 minutes. Remove to wire racks; cool completely.

VARIATION: You can substitute 1 package (6 ounces) of tropical medley dried chopped fruit for the mangoes, apples and cherries.

Triple Ginger Cookies

2 cups all-purpose flour

2 teaspoons baking soda

1 teaspoon ground ginger

½ teaspoon salt

¾ cup (1½ sticks) unsalted butter

1¼ cups granulated sugar, divided

¼ cup molasses

1 egg

1 tablespoon finely minced fresh ginger

1 tablespoon finely minced crystallized ginger*

Look for softer, larger slices of ginger at natural foods or specialty stores. If using the small dry cubes of ginger, steep the cubes in boiling hot water a few minutes to soften, then drain, pat dry and mince.

1. Combine flour, baking soda, ground ginger and salt in medium bowl.

2. Melt butter in small heavy saucepan over low heat; pour into large bowl and cool slightly. Add 1 cup sugar, molasses and egg; beat with electric mixer at medium speed until well blended. Gradually add flour mixture at low speed, beating just until blended. Add fresh ginger and crystallized ginger; mix just until blended. Cover; refrigerate 1 hour.

3. Preheat oven to 375°F. Line cookie sheets with parchment paper or lightly grease. Place remaining ¼ cup sugar in small bowl. Roll dough into 1-inch balls; roll in sugar. Place 3 inches apart on prepared cookie sheets. (If dough is very sticky, drop by teaspoonfuls into sugar to coat.)

4. For chewy cookies, bake 7 minutes or until edges just start to brown. For crisper cookies, bake 2 to 4 minutes longer. Cool on cookie sheets 1 minute. Remove to wire racks; cool completely.

VARIATION: Roll dough in plastic wrap to form a log. Refrigerate up to 1 week or freeze up to 2 months until needed for baking. To bake, bring the dough nearly to room temperature and slice. Dip the tops in sugar and bake as directed in step 4.

Linzer Sandwich Cookies

1⅔ cups all-purpose flour
¼ teaspoon baking powder
¼ teaspoon salt
¾ cup granulated sugar
½ cup (1 stick) unsalted butter, softened

1 egg
1 teaspoon vanilla
Powdered sugar (optional)
Seedless red raspberry jam

1. Combine flour, baking powder and salt in medium bowl. Beat granulated sugar and butter in large bowl with electric mixer at medium speed until light and fluffy. Beat in egg and vanilla until blended. Gradually add flour mixture at low speed, beating just until blended. Divide dough in half. Wrap each half in plastic wrap; refrigerate 2 hours or until firm.

2. Preheat oven to 375°F. Roll out half of dough on lightly floured surface to ³⁄₁₆-inch thickness. Cut out circles with 1½-inch floured scalloped or plain round cookie cutters. (If dough becomes too soft, refrigerate several minutes before continuing.) Place cutouts 2 inches apart on ungreased cookie sheets.

3. Roll out remaining half of dough and cut out circles. Cut 1-inch centers of different shapes from circles. Place 2 inches apart on ungreased cookie sheets.

4. Bake 7 to 9 minutes or until edges are lightly browned. Cool cookies on cookie sheets 2 minutes. Remove cookies to wire racks; cool completely.

5. Sprinkle powdered sugar over cookies with holes, if desired. Spread jam on flat sides of whole cookies; top with cut out cookies. Store tightly covered at room temperature or freeze up to 3 months.

Oatmeal Apricot Ginger Cookies

MAKES 2 DOZEN COOKIES

1¼ cups old-fashioned rolled oats
½ cup all-purpose flour
1½ teaspoons ground ginger
¾ teaspoon baking soda
½ teaspoon salt
½ cup granulated sugar

¼ cup packed brown sugar
¼ cup (½ stick) unsalted butter, softened
2 tablespoons canola oil
1 egg
6 ounces whole dried apricots, chopped

1. Preheat oven to 375°F. Line cookie sheets with parchment paper. Combine oats, flour, ginger, baking soda and salt in medium bowl.

2. Beat granulated sugar, brown sugar, butter and oil in large bowl with electric mixer at medium-high speed until light and fluffy. Add egg; beat until well blended. Gradually add oat mixture at low speed, beating just until blended. Stir in apricots.

3. Drop dough by tablespoonfuls 3 inches apart on prepared cookie sheets (six cookies per sheet).

4. Bake 8 minutes or until slightly golden on edges and light in the middle. (Cookies will not look done at this point, but will continue to cook while cooling.) Cool on cookie sheets 3 minutes. Remove to wire rack; cool completely.

Nutmeg Molasses Cookies

MAKES ABOUT 5 DOZEN COOKIES

3 cups all-purpose flour

2 teaspoons baking soda

1 teaspoon ground nutmeg

1 teaspoon ground cinnamon

½ teaspoon salt

1½ cups granulated sugar, plus additional for decorating

1 cup shortening

⅓ cup molasses

1 teaspoon vanilla

2 eggs

1. Preheat oven to 350°F. Combine flour, baking soda, nutmeg, cinnamon and salt in medium bowl.

2. Beat 1½ cups sugar, shortening, molasses and vanilla in large bowl with electric mixer at medium speed until creamy. Add eggs, one at a time, beating well after each addition. Gradually add flour mixture at low speed, beating just until blended. Beat at medium speed until thick dough forms.

3. Shape dough into 1½-inch balls. Place 3 inches apart on ungreased cookie sheets. Flatten with bottom of glass dipped in sugar.

4. Bake 10 minutes or until cookies look dry. Remove to wire racks; cool completely on wire racks.

Chocolate Fruit & Nut Cookies

1¼ cups all-purpose flour

¼ cup unsweetened cocoa powder

½ teaspoon salt

½ teaspoon baking soda

½ cup (1 stick) unsalted butter, softened

½ cup granulated sugar

¼ cup packed brown sugar

¼ cup vegetable oil

1 egg

1 teaspoon vanilla

½ cup old-fashioned oats

¾ cup mixed dried fruit bits

¾ cup semisweet chocolate chunks

½ cup chopped mixed nuts

1. Preheat oven to 350°F. Grease cookie sheets or line with parchment paper. Combine flour, cocoa, salt and baking soda in medium bowl.

2. Beat butter, granulated sugar and brown sugar in large bowl until light and fluffy. Add oil, egg and vanilla; beat until well blended. Add flour mixture and oats; beat on low speed just until blended. Stir in fruit bits, chocolate chunks and chopped nuts.

3. Shape dough by heaping tablespoons into balls; place 2 inches apart on prepared cookie sheets.

4. Bake 12 minutes or until set and no longer shiny. Cool on cookie sheets 2 minutes. Remove to wire racks; cool completely.

Date Pinwheel Cookies

MAKES 6 DOZEN COOKIES

1¼ cups pitted dates, finely chopped

¾ cup orange juice

½ cup granulated sugar

1 tablespoon unsalted butter

3 cups plus 1 tablespoon all-purpose flour, divided

2 teaspoons vanilla, divided

1 cup packed brown sugar

4 ounces cream cheese, softened

¼ cup shortening

2 eggs

1 teaspoon baking soda

½ teaspoon salt

1. Combine dates, orange juice, granulated sugar, butter and 1 tablespoon flour in medium saucepan over medium heat. Cook 10 minutes or until thick, stirring frequently. Remove from heat. Stir in 1 teaspoon vanilla; set aside to cool.

2. Beat brown sugar, cream cheese and shortening in large bowl with electric mixer at medium speed about 3 minutes or until creamy. Add eggs and remaining 1 teaspoon vanilla; beat 2 minutes.

3. Combine remaining 3 cups flour, baking soda and salt in medium bowl. Add to shortening mixture; stir just until blended. Divide dough in half. Roll one half of dough on lightly floured surface into 12X9-inch rectangle. Spread half of date mixture evenly over dough, leaving ¼-inch border at top short edge. Starting at opposite end, tightly roll up dough jelly-roll style. Wrap in plastic wrap; freeze at least 1 hour. Repeat with remaining dough and date mixture.

4. Preheat oven to 350°F. Grease cookie sheets or line with parchment paper. Cut dough into ¼-inch slices. Place slices 1 inch apart on prepared cookie sheets.

5. Bake 12 minutes or until lightly browned. Cool on cookie sheets 2 minutes. Remove to wire racks; cool completely.

Gingerbread Bears

3½ cups all-purpose flour
2 teaspoons ground cinnamon
1½ teaspoons ground ginger
1 teaspoon salt
1 teaspoon baking soda
1 teaspoon ground allspice
1 cup (2 sticks) unsalted butter, softened
1 cup packed brown sugar

1 teaspoon vanilla
⅓ cup molasses
2 eggs
Assorted nonpareils (optional)
Buttercream Frosting (recipe follows) or prepared canned frosting (optional)
Colored sugars and assorted candies (optional)

1. Combine flour, cinnamon, ginger, salt, baking soda and allspice in medium bowl. Beat butter, brown sugar and vanilla in large bowl with electric mixer at medium speed about 5 minutes or until light and fluffy. Beat in molasses and eggs until well blended. Beat in flour mixture at low speed until well blended. Divide dough into 3 equal pieces; cover and refrigerate at least 2 hours or up to 24 hours.

2. Preheat oven to 350°F. Grease large cookie sheets or line with parchment paper. Working with 1 piece at a time, roll dough on lightly floured surface to ⅛-inch thickness. Cut dough with 3-inch bear-shaped cookie cutter. Place cutouts 1 inch apart on prepared cookie sheets. Shape dough scraps into small balls and ropes to make noses and ears, and to decorate bears.

3. Bake 10 minutes or until edges are lightly browned. Cool on cookie sheets 1 minute. Remove to wire racks; cool completely.

4. Prepare Buttercream Frosting, if desired. Tint icing with desired colors. Pipe or spread frosting on cookies. Decorate with assorted nonpareils, colored sugars and assorted candies, if desired.

Buttercream Frosting

MAKES ABOUT 2 CUPS

½ cup (1 stick) unsalted butter, softened

1 box (16 ounces) powdered sugar, sifted

2 tablespoons milk

1 teaspoon vanilla

Beat butter and powdered sugar in large bowl with electric mixer at low speed until blended. Add milk and vanilla; beat at medium speed until frosting is of desired spreading or piping consistency.

Tangy Cherry Cookies

MAKES 3 DOZEN COOKIES

1¾ cups all-purpose flour
½ cup fine cornmeal
1 teaspoon dried lemon peel
½ teaspoon baking powder
½ teaspoon salt
1 cup (2 sticks) unsalted butter, softened

½ cup granulated sugar
½ cup packed brown sugar
1 egg
1½ teaspoons vanilla
¾ cup dried cherries
Coarse sugar (optional)

1. Combine flour, cornmeal, lemon peel, baking powder and salt in medium bowl; mix well.

2. Beat butter, granulated sugar and brown sugar in large bowl with electric mixer at medium-high speed until light and fluffy. Add egg and vanilla; beat until well blended. With mixer running on low speed, gradually add flour mixture beating just until blended. Stir in cherries.

3. Roll dough into two logs, each 6 inches long and 2 inches in diameter. Wrap tightly in plastic wrap; refrigerate 2 hours or until firm.

4. Preheat oven to 350°F. Line cookie sheets with parchment paper. Cut each log crosswise into 18 (¼-inch) slices with serrated knife. Place 1 inch apart on prepared cookie sheets. Sprinkle with coarse sugar, if desired.

5. Bake 15 to 20 minutes or until edges are golden brown. Cool on cookie sheets 10 minutes. Remove to wire racks; cool completely.

Eggnog Cookies

2¼ cups all-purpose flour

1 teaspoon baking powder

1 teaspoon ground cinnamon

1 teaspoon freshly grated nutmeg or ground nutmeg

½ teaspoon salt

1¼ cups granulated sugar

¾ cup (1½ sticks) unsalted butter, softened

½ cup eggnog (no alcohol added)

2 egg yolks

1 teaspoon vanilla

Additional freshly grated nutmeg

1. Preheat oven to 300°F. Combine flour, baking powder, cinnamon, 1 teaspoon nutmeg and salt in medium bowl.

2. Beat sugar and butter in large bowl with electric mixer at medium speed until light and fluffy. Beat in eggnog, egg yolks and vanilla. Gradually add flour mixture at low speed, beating just until blended after each addition.

3. Drop dough by rounded teaspoonfuls 2 inches apart onto ungreased cookie sheets. Sprinkle with additional nutmeg.

4. Bake 20 minutes or until bottoms are lightly browned. Remove to wire racks; cool completely.

FILLED & FANCY TREATS

Marshmallow Sandwich Cookies

2 cups all-purpose flour

½ cup unsweetened cocoa powder

2 teaspoons baking soda

½ teaspoon salt

1½ cups sugar, divided

⅔ cup (10 tablespoons) unsalted butter, softened

¼ cup light corn syrup

1 egg

1 teaspoon vanilla

24 large marshmallows

1. Preheat oven to 350°F. Combine flour, cocoa, baking soda and salt in medium bowl.

2. Beat 1¼ cups sugar and butter in large bowl with electric mixer at medium-high speed until light and fluffy. Beat in corn syrup, egg and vanilla until blended. Gradually add flour mixture, beating at low speed just until blended. Cover and refrigerate 15 minutes or until dough is firm enough to shape into balls.

3. Place remaining ¼ cup sugar in small bowl. Shape dough into 1-inch balls; roll in sugar to coat. Place cookies 3 inches apart on ungreased cookie sheets.

4. Bake 10 to 11 minutes or until set. Cool on cookie sheets 3 minutes. Remove to wire racks; cool completely.

5. Place one cookie on microwavable plate. Top with one marshmallow. Microwave on HIGH about 10 seconds or until marshmallow is softened. Immediately place another cookie, flat side down, on top of hot marshmallow; press together. Repeat with remaining cookies and marshmallows.

Chocolate-Topped Linzer Cookies

3 cups hazelnuts, toasted,* skins removed, divided

1 cup (2 sticks) unsalted butter, softened

1 cup powdered sugar

½ teaspoon grated lemon peel

¼ teaspoon salt

½ egg**

3 cups sifted all-purpose flour

½ cup chocolate-hazelnut spread

½ cup seedless red raspberry jam

6 ounces semisweet chocolate

2 tablespoons shortening

*To toast haznuts, place in single layer on ungreased baking sheet. Bake in preheated 350°F oven 8 to 10 minutes or until lightly browned, stirring occasionally. Place nuts in clean kitchen towel; rub to remove skins.

**To measure ½ egg, lightly beat 1 egg in glass measuring cup; remove half, about 2 tablespoons, for use in recipe.

1. Place 1½ cups hazelnuts in food processor; process until finely ground. (There should be ½ cup ground nuts; if necessary, process additional nuts.) Set aside remaining whole nuts for garnish.

2. Beat butter, powdered sugar, lemon peel and salt in large bowl with electric mixer at medium speed just until blended. *Do not overmix.* Add egg; beat until well blended. Stir in ground hazelnuts. Gradually add flour at low speed, beating just until blended. Divide dough into quarters. Wrap each piece in plastic wrap; refrigerate about 2 hours or until firm.

3. Preheat oven to 350°F. Line cookie sheets with parchment paper. Working with one piece at a time, roll out dough to ⅛- to ¹⁄₁₆-inch thickness on lightly floured surface. Cut out circles with 1¼-inch round cookie cutter. Place 1 inch apart on prepared cookie sheets.

4. Bake 7 to 8 minutes or until lightly browned. Cool completely on cookie sheets.

5. Spread one third of cookies lightly with chocolate-hazelnut spread. Top with plain cookies; press gently.

6. Spoon raspberry jam into pastry bag fitted with ⅓-inch round tip. Pipe about ⅓ teaspoon jam onto centers of second cookie layers. Top with plain cookies; press gently. Let cookies stand about 1 hour.

7. Melt chocolate and shortening in small heavy saucepan over low heat; stir until smooth. Press cookie layers lightly together. Dip top of each cookie into chocolate mixture just to cover. Shake to remove excess chocolate. Place cookies on wire racks; press whole hazelnut on top of each cookie. Let stand until chocolate is set.

Chocolate Tassies

CRUST

- 1 cup (2 sticks) unsalted cold butter, cut into chunks
- 6 ounces cold cream cheese, cut into chunks
- ½ teaspoon salt
- 2 cups all-purpose flour

FILLING

- 2 tablespoons unsalted butter
- 2 ounces unsweetened chocolate
- 1½ cups packed brown sugar
- 2 eggs
- 2 teaspoons vanilla
- ¼ teaspoon salt
- 1½ cups chopped pecans

1. For crust, beat butter, cream cheese and ½ teaspoon salt in large bowl with electric mixer at medium speed until light and fluffy. Stir in flour until blended. Cover and refrigerate 1 hour.

2. Preheat oven to 350°F. Divide dough into four pieces. Shape one piece into smooth ball on lightly floured surface; divide into 12 balls. Press each ball into bottom and up side of mini (1¾-inch) muffin pan cup. Repeat with remaining dough. (If reusing muffin pan, let pan cool completely between batches and keep dough refrigerated until ready to use).

3. For filling, melt 2 tablespoons butter and chocolate in medium heavy saucepan over low heat. Remove from heat; stir in brown sugar, eggs, vanilla and ¼ teaspoon salt until well blended and thick. Stir in pecans. Spoon about 1 teaspoon filling into each crust.

4. Bake 20 to 25 minutes or until crusts are golden brown and filling is set. Cool completely in pan on wire rack. Loosen cups with small metal spatula or knife; remove from pan.

Coconut Cups

CRUST

- 1 cup (2 sticks) unsalted butter, softened
- 6 ounces cream cheese, softened
- ½ teaspoon salt
- 2 cups all-purpose flour

FILLING

- 1 can (14 ounces) sweetened condensed milk
- 2 eggs
- 1½ teaspoons vanilla
- ½ teaspoon almond extract
- 1⅓ cups flaked or shredded coconut

1. For crust, beat butter, cream cheese and ½ teaspoon salt in large bowl with electric mixer at medium speed until light and fluffy. Stir in flour until blended. Cover and refrigerate 1 hour.

2. Preheat oven to 375°F. Divide dough into four pieces. Shape one piece into smooth ball on lightly floured surface; divide into 12 balls. Press each ball into bottom and up side of mini (1¾-inch) muffin pan cup. Repeat with remaining dough. (If reusing muffin pan, let pan cool completely between batches and keep dough refrigerated until ready to use).

3. For filling, combine condensed milk, eggs, vanilla and almond extract in medium bowl; mix well. Stir in coconut. Fill muffin cups three-fourths full.

4. Bake 16 to 18 minutes or until slightly browned. Cool completely in pan on wire rack. Loosen cups with small metal spatula or knife; remove from pan.

CHOCOLATE COCONUT CUPS: Add ¼ cup unsweetened cocoa powder to filling with eggs; proceed as directed.

Black & White Sandwich Cookies

COOKIES

- 1¼ cups (2½ sticks) unsalted butter, softened
- ¾ cup superfine or granulated sugar
- 1 egg
- 1½ teaspoons vanilla
- ¼ teaspoon salt
- 2⅓ cups all-purpose flour, divided
- ⅓ cup unsweetened cocoa powder

FILLING

- ½ cup (1 stick) unsalted butter, softened
- 4 ounces cream cheese, at room temperature
- 2 cups plus 2 tablespoons powdered sugar
- 2 tablespoons unsweetened cocoa powder

1. For cookies, beat 1¼ cups butter and superfine sugar in large bowl with electric mixer until creamy. Beat in egg, vanilla and salt until well blended. Gradually add 2 cups flour at low speed, beating just until blended.

2. Remove half of dough to medium bowl; stir in remaining ⅓ cup flour. Add ⅓ cup cocoa to dough in mixer bowl; beat just until blended. Wrap doughs separately in plastic wrap; refrigerate 30 minutes or until firm.

3. Preheat oven to 350°F. Grease cookie sheets or line with parchment paper. Roll out plain dough on floured surface to ¼-inch thickness. Cut out 2-inch circles; place 2 inches apart on prepared cookie sheets. Repeat with chocolate dough.

4. Bake 8 to 10 minutes. Remove to wire racks; cool completely.

5. For filling, beat ½ cup butter and cream cheese in medium bowl with electric mixer until well blended. Add 2 cups powdered sugar; beat until creamy. Remove half of filling to small bowl; stir in remaining 2 tablespoons powdered sugar. Add 2 tablespoons cocoa to filling in mixer bowl; beat until smooth.

6. Pipe or spread chocolate frosting on flat side of half of plain cookies; top with remaining plain cookies. Pipe or spread vanilla frosting on flat side of half of chocolate cookies; top with remaining chocolate cookies.

Chocolate Macarons

MAKES 16 TO 20 MACARON SANDWICHES

1 cup powdered sugar

⅔ cup blanched almond flour*

3 tablespoons unsweetened cocoa powder

3 egg whites, at room temperature*

¼ cup granulated sugar

Chocolate Ganache (page 139), chocolate-hazelnut spread or raspberry jam

*For best results, separate the eggs while cold. Leave the egg whites at room temperature for 3 or 4 hours. Reserve yolks in refrigerator for another use.

1. Line two baking sheets with parchment paper. Double baking sheets by placing another sheet underneath each to protect macarons from burning or cracking. (Do NOT use insulated baking sheets.)

2. Place powdered sugar, almond flour and cocoa in food processor. Pulse 2 to 3 minutes or until well combined into very fine powder, scraping bowl occasionally. Sift mixture twice. Discard any remaining large pieces.

3. Beat egg whites in large bowl with electric mixer at high speed until foamy. Gradually add granulated sugar, beating at high speed 2 to 3 minutes or until mixture forms stiff, shiny peaks, scraping bowl occasionally.

4. Add half of flour mixture to egg whites. Stir with spatula to combine (about 12 strokes). Repeat with remaining flour mixture. Mix about 15 strokes more by pressing against side of bowl and scooping from bottom until batter is smooth and shiny. Check consistency by dropping spoonful of batter onto plate. It should have a peak which quickly relaxes back into batter. *Do not overmix or undermix.*

5. Attach ½-inch plain piping tip to pastry bag. Scoop batter into bag. Pipe 1-inch circles about 2 inches apart onto prepared baking sheets. Rap baking sheet on flat surface to remove air bubbles and set aside. Repeat with remaining batter. Let macarons rest, uncovered, until tops harden slightly; this takes from 15 minutes on dry days to 1 hour in more humid conditions. Gently touch top of macaron to check. When batter does not stick, macarons are ready to bake.

6. Meanwhile, preheat oven to 375°F.** Place oven rack in center. Place one sheet of macarons in oven. After 5 minutes, reduce heat to 325°F. Bake 10 to 13 minutes, checking at 5-minute intervals. If macarons begin to brown, cover loosely with foil and reduce oven temperature or prop oven open slightly with wooden spoon. Repeat with remaining baking sheet.

7. Cool completely on baking sheet on wire rack. While cooling, if cookies appear to be sticking to parchment, lift parchment edges and spray pan underneath lightly with water. Steam will help release macarons.

8. Meanwhile, prepare Chocolate Ganache. Match same size cookies; spread bottom macaron with Chocolate Ganache and top with another. Store macarons in covered container in refrigerator 4 to 5 days. Freeze for longer storage.

**Oven temperature is crucial. Use an oven thermometer, if possible.

CHOCOLATE GANACHE: Place 4 ounces chopped semisweet or bittersweet chocolate in shallow bowl. Heat ½ cup whipping cream in small saucepan until bubbles form around edges. Pour cream over chocolate; let stand 5 minutes. Stir until smooth.

Chocolate-Hazelnut Sandwich Cookies

MAKES 30 SANDWICH COOKIES

¾ cup (1½ sticks) unsalted
  butter, slightly softened
¾ cup granulated sugar
3 egg yolks
1 teaspoon vanilla

2 cups all-purpose flour
½ teaspoon salt
⅔ cup chocolate-hazelnut
  spread

1. Beat butter and sugar in large bowl with electric mixer at medium speed 1 minute. Beat in egg yolks and vanilla until well blended. Add flour and salt; beat on low speed just until combined. Divide dough in half. Shape each piece into 6X1½-inch log. Wrap in plastic wrap; refrigerate at least 2 hours or until firm.

2. Preheat oven to 350°F. Line cookie sheets with parchment paper. Cut dough into ⅛-inch-thick slices; place 1 inch apart on prepared cookie sheets.

3. Bake 10 to 12 minutes or until edges are light brown. Cool on cookie sheets 5 minutes. Remove to wire racks; cool completely.

4. Spread 1 teaspoon hazelnut spread on flat side of half of cookies; top with remaining cookies. Store covered in airtight container.

NOTE: The dough can be refrigerated up to 3 days or may be frozen for up to 1 month.

Gooey Thumbprints

1 cup (2 sticks) unsalted butter, softened
½ cup powdered sugar
2 tablespoons packed brown sugar
¼ teaspoon salt
1 egg
2 cups all-purpose flour
¼ cup seedless strawberry, grape or apricot jam

1. Beat butter, powdered sugar, brown sugar and salt in large bowl with electric mixer at medium speed until light and fluffy. Add egg; beat until well blended.

2. Add flour, ½ cup at a time, beating on low speed after each addition. Shape dough into a disc; wrap tightly in plastic wrap. Refrigerate at least 1 hour or until firm.

3. Preheat oven to 300°F. Shape dough into 1-inch balls; place 1 inch apart on ungreased cookie sheets. Make small indentation in each ball with thumb; fill with heaping ¼ teaspoon jam.

4. Bake 25 to 27 minutes or until tops of cookies are light golden brown. Cool on cookie sheets 1 minute. Remove to wire racks; cool completely.

Apricot-Pecan Tassies

MAKES 2 DOZEN COOKIES

1 cup all-purpose flour
½ cup (1 stick) plus
    1 tablespoon unsalted
    butter, cut into pieces,
    divided
6 tablespoons cream cheese
½ teaspoon salt, divided

¾ cup packed brown sugar
1 egg
½ teaspoon vanilla
⅔ cup diced dried apricots
⅓ cup chopped pecans

1. Place flour, ½ cup butter, cream cheese and ¼ teaspoon salt in food processor; pulse until mixture forms a ball. Wrap dough in plastic wrap; refrigerate 15 minutes.

2. Preheat oven to 325°F. Grease 24 mini (1¾-inch) muffin cups or line with paper baking cups.

3. Beat brown sugar, egg, remaining 1 tablespoon butter, vanilla and remaining ¼ teaspoon salt in large bowl with electric mixer at medium speed until creamy. Stir in apricots and pecans.

4. Shape dough into 24 balls; place in prepared muffin cups. Press dough onto bottom and up side of each cup. Spoon about 1 teaspoon apricot mixture into each crust.

5. Bake 25 minutes or until light golden brown. Cool completely in pans on wire racks.

Pistachio Cookie Cups

½ cup (1 stick) plus 1 tablespoon unsalted butter, softened, divided

3 ounces cream cheese, softened

2 tablespoons granulated sugar

½ teaspoon salt, divided

1 cup all-purpose flour

½ teaspoon grated orange peel

1 cup powdered sugar, plus additional for serving

½ cup chopped pistachio nuts

⅓ cup dried cranberries

1 egg

½ teaspoon orange extract

1. Beat ½ cup butter, cream cheese, granulated sugar and ¼ teaspoon salt in large bowl with electric mixer at medium speed until light and fluffy. Add flour and orange peel; beat just until blended. Shape dough into a ball; wrap in plastic wrap. Freeze 30 minutes.

2. Combine 1 cup powdered sugar, pistachios, cranberries, egg, remaining 1 tablespoon butter, orange extract and remaining and ¼ teaspoon salt in medium bowl; stir until well blended.

3. Preheat oven to 350°F. Lightly grease 24 mini (1¾-inch) muffin cups. Press 1 tablespoon dough onto bottom and up side of each muffin cup. Fill shells three-fourths full with pistachio mixture.

4. Bake 25 minutes or until filling is set. Remove cookie cups to wire racks; cool completely. Sprinkle with additional powdered sugar, if desired.

Double Chocolate Sandwich Cookies

1⅔ cups all-purpose flour

¼ teaspoon baking powder

¼ teaspoon salt

¾ cup granulated sugar

½ cup (1 stick) plus 2 teaspoons unsalted butter, softened, divided

1 egg

1 teaspoon vanilla

4 ounces bittersweet chocolate, chopped

¾ cup milk chocolate chips

1. Combine flour, baking powder and salt in medium bowl. Beat granulated sugar and ½ cup butter in large bowl with electric mixer at medium speed until light and fluffy. Beat in egg and vanilla until blended. Gradually add flour mixture, beating at low speed until dough forms. Divide dough in half. Wrap each half in plastic wrap; refrigerate 2 hours or until firm.

2. Preheat oven to 350°F. Line cookie sheets with parchment paper. Unwrap dough. Roll out dough on lightly floured surface ¼-inch thick. Cut circles with 1½-inch round cookie cutter. Cut ½-inch circles out of half of circles. Place cutouts on prepared baking sheets.

3. Bake 10 to 12 minutes or until edges are lightly browned. Cool on cookie sheets 2 minutes. Remove to wire racks; cool completely.

4. Heat bittersweet chocolate and 2 teaspoons butter in small heavy saucepan over low heat, stirring frequently, until chocolate is melted. Spread chocolate over flat sides of cookies without holes; immediately top with cutout cookies.

5. Place milk chocolate chips in resealable food storage bag; seal bag. Microwave on MEDIUM (50%) 1½ minutes. Turn bag over; microwave 1 to 1½ minutes more or until chocolate is melted. Knead bag until chocolate is smooth.

6. Cut tiny corner off bag; drizzle chocolate decoratively over sandwich cookies. Let stand about 30 minutes or until chocolate is set.

Cream Cheese Cookies

1 package (8 ounces) cream cheese, softened
½ cup shortening
½ cup (1 stick) unsalted butter, softened
¼ teaspoon salt
3 cups all-purpose flour
Powdered sugar
Apricot jam, raspberry jam and/or mixed berry jam

1. Beat cream cheese, shortening, butter and salt in large bowl with electric mixer at medium speed until creamy. Gradually add flour at low speed, beating until well blended. Shape dough into a disc. Wrap tightly in plastic wrap; refrigerate 2 hours until firm or overnight.

2. Preheat oven to 375°F.

3. Roll out dough to ⅛-inch thickness on surface dusted with powdered sugar. Cut out circles with 1½-inch round cookie cutter. Place scant ¼ teaspoon filling in center of each circle. Bring two edges over center of cookie and pinch together. Place on ungreased cookie sheets.

4. Bake 15 to 17 minutes or until light golden brown. Remove to wire racks; cool completely. Dust with powdered sugar, if desired.

Eggnog Sandwich Cookies

COOKIES

- 1 cup (2 sticks) unsalted butter, softened
- 1¼ cups plus 1 tablespoon granulated sugar, divided
- 1 egg yolk
- ½ cup sour cream
- ¼ teaspoon salt
- 2½ cups all-purpose flour
- ½ teaspoon grated nutmeg
- ¼ teaspoon ground ginger

FILLING

- ½ cup (1 stick) unsalted butter, softened
- ¼ cup shortening
- 2½ cups powdered sugar
- 2 tablespoons brandy or milk

1. Preheat oven to 350°F. Grease cookie sheets or line with parchment paper.

2. Beat 1 cup butter and 1¼ cups granulated sugar in large bowl with electric mixer at medium speed until light and fluffy. Add egg yolk; beat until blended. Add sour cream and salt; beat until well blended. Gradually add flour to butter mixture, beating until well blended.

3. Shape teaspoonfuls of dough into balls. Place on prepared cookie sheets; flatten slightly. Combine remaining 1 tablespoon granulated sugar, nutmeg and ginger in small bowl; sprinkle over cookies.

4. Bake 12 minutes or until edges are golden. Cool on cookie sheets 5 minutes. Remove to wire racks; cool completely.

5. For filling, beat ½ cup butter and shortening in large bowl with electric mixer at medium speed until light and fluffy. Add powdered sugar and brandy; beat until well blended. Spread or pipe filling on flat side of half of cookies. Top with remaining cookies, flat side down.

BEST BARS & BROWNIES

Double Chocolate Dream Bars

2¼ cups all-purpose flour, divided

1 cup (2 sticks) unsalted butter, softened

¾ cup powdered sugar, plus additional for garnish

⅓ cup unsweetened cocoa powder

½ teaspoon salt

2 cups granulated sugar

4 eggs

4 ounces unsweetened chocolate, melted

1. Preheat oven to 350°F. Line 13×9-inch baking pan with parchment paper.

2. Beat 2 cups flour, butter, ¾ cup powdered sugar, cocoa and salt in large bowl with electric mixer at low speed until blended. Beat at medium speed until well blended and stiff dough forms. Press firmly into prepared pan. Bake 15 to 20 minutes or just until set. *Do not overbake.*

3. Meanwhile, combine remaining ¼ cup flour and granulated sugar in large bowl. Add eggs and melted chocolate; beat with electric mixer at medium-high speed until well blended. Pour over crust.

4. Bake 25 minutes or until center is firm to the touch. Cool completely in pan on wire rack. Sprinkle with additional powdered sugar, if desired. Cut into bars.

Dark Chocolate Nut Bars

MAKES ABOUT 4 DOZEN BARS

1 package (12 ounces) dark chocolate nuggets with almonds*

1½ cups all-purpose flour

⅓ cup unsweetened cocoa powder

1½ teaspoons baking powder

½ teaspoon salt

1 cup (2 sticks) unsalted butter, softened

¾ cup packed brown sugar

½ cup granulated sugar

2 eggs

1 teaspoon vanilla

1 cup chopped pecans

Or substitute any chocolate candy bars, enough to make 1½ cups chopped candy.

1. Preheat oven to 350°F. Grease 13X9-inch baking pan. Chop candy into ¼-inch chunks; refrigerate until ready to use.

2. Combine flour, cocoa, baking powder and salt in small bowl. Beat butter, brown sugar and granulated sugar in large bowl with electric mixer at medium speed until creamy. Beat in eggs and vanilla until well blended. Gradually add flour at low speed, beating just until blended.

3. Reserve half of chopped candy; stir remaining candy and pecans into dough. Spread dough in prepared pan. Sprinkle with reserved candy.

4. Bake about 25 minutes or until toothpick inserted into center comes out clean. Cool completely in pan on wire rack. Cut into 1½-inch squares.

Polish Honey Bars

½ cup granulated sugar, divided
2 tablespoons boiling water
⅓ cup honey
2 tablespoons unsalted butter
1 teaspoon ground allspice
½ teaspoon ground cinnamon
¼ teaspoon ground cloves
¼ teaspoon ground nutmeg
¼ teaspoon salt
2 cups all-purpose flour
3 tablespoons cold water
1 egg
1 teaspoon baking soda
Chocolate Filling (page 159)
1 cup semisweet chocolate chips
32 whole almonds

1. Combine 2 tablespoons sugar and boiling water in small heavy saucepan over medium heat; stir until dissolved and slightly brown. Add remaining sugar, honey, butter, allspice, cinnamon, cloves, nutmeg and salt; bring to a boil over high heat, stirring constantly. Remove saucepan from heat; pour mixture into medium bowl. Cool slightly.

2. Add flour, cold water, egg and baking soda to cooled sugar mixture; stir with spoon until well blended. Cover; let stand 20 minutes.

3. Preheat oven to 350°F. Grease and flour 15X10-inch sheet pan. Roll out dough on lightly floured surface with lightly floured rolling pin to almost fit size of pan. Press dough evenly into pan to edges. Bake 10 to 13 minutes or until cookie springs back when lightly touched in center. Cool completely in pan on wire rack.

4. Run knife around edge of cookie to loosen. Place wire rack top side down over pan; flip rack and pan over together; remove pan. Cut cookie in half crosswise to form two rectangles.

5. Prepare Chocolate Filling; spread evenly over one rectangle. Top with other rectangle, flat side up. Wrap cookie sandwich in plastic wrap. Place baking sheet on top of cookie sandwich; place heavy cans or other weights on baking sheet. Let stand overnight.

6. Microwave chocolate chips in medium microwavable bowl on MEDIUM (50%) 2 to 3 minutes, stirring at 30-second intervals until melted and smooth. Dip wide part of each almond into chocolate; place dipped almonds on waxed paper to set.

7. Remove weights and baking sheet from cookie sandwich; unwrap. Spread remaining melted chocolate over top. Before chocolate sets, score top of cookie sandwich into 32 bars. Place 1 dipped almond on each bar. Let stand at room temperature until set; cut into bars.

Chocolate Filling

MAKES ABOUT 1 CUP FILLING

1 cup whole almonds
¼ cup whipping cream
½ cup semisweet chocolate
   chips

¾ cup powdered sugar, divided
½ teaspoon vanilla

1. Preheat oven to 350°F. Spread almonds on baking sheet. Bake 5 to 7 minutes or until lightly browned and fragrant, stirring frequently. Cool completely. Place in food processor; pulse until nuts are finely ground but not pasty.

2. Heat cream and chocolate chips in small saucepan over medium heat until melted and smooth, stirring constantly. Remove from heat; stir in almonds, ½ cup powdered sugar and vanilla with spoon. Stir in additional powdered sugar until filling is stiff enough to spread.

Apricot Oatmeal Bars

MAKES 12 TO 16 BARS

1½ cups old-fashioned oats
1¼ cups all-purpose flour
½ cup packed brown sugar
1 teaspoon ground ginger, divided
½ teaspoon baking soda
½ teaspoon salt
½ teaspoon ground cinnamon
¾ cup (1½ sticks) unsalted butter, melted
1¼ cups apricot preserves

1. Preheat oven to 350°F. Line 8-inch square baking pan with foil.

2. Combine oats, flour, brown sugar, ½ teaspoon ginger, baking soda, salt and cinnamon in large bowl. Add butter; stir just until moistened and crumbly. Reserve 1½ cups oat mixture for topping. Press remaining oat mixture evenly onto bottom of prepared pan.

3. Combine preserves and remaining ½ teaspoon ginger in small bowl. Spread preserves evenly over crust; sprinkle with reserved oat mixture.

4. Bake 30 minutes or until golden brown. Cool completely in pan on wire rack. Cut into bars.

Chocolate Pecan Bars

CRUST

1 1/3 cups all-purpose flour

1/2 cup (1 stick) unsalted butter, softened

1/4 cup packed brown sugar

1/2 teaspoon salt

TOPPING

3 eggs

3/4 cup light corn syrup

2 tablespoons unsalted butter, melted and cooled

1/2 teaspoon vanilla

1/2 teaspoon almond extract

3/4 cup milk chocolate chips

3/4 cup semisweet chocolate chips

3/4 cup chopped pecans, toasted*

3/4 cup granulated sugar

To toast pecans, spread on baking sheet. Bake in preheated 350°F oven 5 to 7 minutes or until lightly browned and fragrant, stirring frequently.

1. Preheat oven to 350°F. Grease 13X9-inch baking pan.

2. For crust, combine flour, 1/2 cup butter, brown sugar and salt in medium bowl; mix with fork until crumbly. Press into bottom of prepared baking pan. Bake 12 to 15 minutes or until lightly browned. Let stand 10 minutes.

3. Meanwhile for topping, place eggs in large bowl; lightly beat with fork. Add corn syrup, 2 tablespoons butter, vanilla and almond extract in large bowl; stir with fork until well blended (do not beat). Fold in chocolate chips, pecans and granulated sugar until blended. Pour over baked crust.

4. Bake 25 to 30 minutes or until toothpick inserted into center comes out clean. Cool completely in pan on wire rack. Cut into bars. Store in refrigerator.

NOTE: For easy removal of corn syrup, first coat the inside of the measuring cup with nonstick cooking spray.

White Chocolate Chunk Brownies

4 ounces unsweetened chocolate, coarsely chopped

½ cup (1 stick) unsalted butter

2 eggs

1¼ cups granulated sugar

1 teaspoon vanilla

½ teaspoon salt

½ cup all-purpose flour

6 ounces white chocolate, cut into ¼-inch pieces

½ cup coarsely chopped walnuts (optional)

1. Preheat oven to 350°F. Grease 8-inch square baking pan or line parchment paper.

2. Melt unsweetened chocolate and butter in small saucepan over low heat, stirring constantly; cool slightly.

3. Beat eggs in large bowl with electric mixer at medium speed 30 seconds. Gradually add sugar, beating at medium speed 4 minutes or until pale and very thick.

4. Add chocolate mixture, vanilla and salt; beat until well blended. Gradually add flour at low speed, beating just until blended. Stir in white chocolate and walnuts, if desired. Spread batter evenly in prepared baking pan.

5. Bake 30 minutes or until center is set and edges just begin to pull away from sides of pan. Cool completely in pan on wire rack. Cut into 2-inch squares.

Linzer Bars

3 cups all-purpose flour

1¾ cups whole almonds, ground*

1½ teaspoons grated lemon peel

1½ teaspoons ground cinnamon

1 teaspoon salt

1¾ cups (3½ sticks) unsalted butter, softened

1 cup granulated sugar

1 egg

¾ cup raspberry preserves

Powdered sugar

Place almonds in food processor. Pulse until nuts are finely ground but not pasty.

1. Preheat oven to 350°F. Grease 13X9-inch baking pan or line with parchment paper. Combine flour, almonds, lemon peel, cinnamon and salt in medium bowl.

2. Beat butter and granulated sugar in large bowl with electric mixer at medium-high speed until light and fluffy. Add egg; beat until blended. Gradually add flour mixture at low speed, beating just until blended.

3. Press 3 cups of dough in bottom of prepared pan. Spread preserves over crust. Press remaining dough, a small amount at a time, evenly over preserves.

4. Bake 40 to 45 minutes or until golden brown. Cool completely in pan on wire rack. Cut into bars; sprinkle with powdered sugar.

Chocolate Chip Shortbread

- ½ cup (1 stick) unsalted butter, softened
- ½ cup granulated sugar
- 2 tablespoons packed brown sugar
- 1 teaspoon vanilla
- 1 cup all-purpose flour
- ½ teaspoon salt
- ½ cup plus 2 tablespoons mini semisweet chocolate chips, divided

1. Preheat oven to 350°F.

2. Beat butter, granulated sugar and brown sugar in large bowl with electric mixer at medium speed until light and fluffy. Beat in vanilla. Add flour and salt; beat at low speed until combined. Stir in ½ cup chocolate chips. Press dough into 8- or 9-inch square baking pan. Sprinkle with remaining 2 tablespoons chocolate chips; press lightly into dough.

3. Bake 15 to 17 minutes or until edges are golden brown. Cool completely in pan on wire rack. Cut into rectangles.

VARIATION: For shortbread wedges, press dough into two 8-inch round baking pans. Bake 12 to 15 minutes or until edges are golden brown and centers are set. Cool completely in pan on wire rack; cut each into 8 wedges.

Seven-Layer Dessert

½ cup (1 stick) unsalted butter, melted

1 teaspoon vanilla

1 cup graham cracker crumbs

1 cup butterscotch chips

1 cup chocolate chips

1 cup shredded coconut

1 cup nuts

1 can (14 ounces) sweetened condensed milk

1. Preheat oven to 350°F.

2. Pour butter into 13X9-inch baking pan. Add vanilla. Sprinkle cracker crumbs over butter. Layer butterscotch chips over crumbs, followed by chocolate chips, coconut and nuts. Pour condensed milk evenly over all.

3. Bake 25 minutes or until lightly browned. Cool completely in pan on wire rack. Cut into bars.

Sour Cream Brownies

½ cup (1 stick) unsalted butter, softened

1 cup packed brown sugar

1 egg

1 cup sour cream

1 teaspoon vanilla

½ cup unsweetened cocoa powder

½ teaspoon baking soda

½ teaspoon salt

2 cups all-purpose flour

1 cup semisweet chocolate chips

Powdered sugar (optional)

1. Preheat oven to 350°F. Grease 13X9-inch baking pan or line with parchment paper.

2. Beat butter and brown sugar in large bowl with electric mixer until creamy. Add egg, sour cream and vanilla; beat until light. Add cocoa, baking soda and salt; beat until smooth. Gradually add flour at low speed, beating until well blended. Stir in chocolate chips. Spread batter evenly in prepared pan.

3. Bake 25 to 30 minutes or until center springs back when lightly touched. Cool completely in pan on wire rack. Cut into bars. Sprinkle with powdered sugar, if desired.

White Chocolate & Almond Brownies

12 ounces white chocolate, broken into pieces

1 cup (2 sticks) unsalted butter

3 eggs

1 teaspoon vanilla

¼ teaspoon salt

¾ cup all-purpose flour

½ cup slivered almonds

1. Preheat oven to 325°F. Grease and flour 9-inch square pan.

2. Melt white chocolate and butter in large heavy saucepan over very low heat, stirring constantly. (White chocolate may separate.) Remove from heat when chocolate is just melted. Transfer to large bowl.

3. Add eggs; beat with electric mixer at medium speed until smooth. Beat in vanilla and salt. Gradually add flour at low speed, beating just until blended. Spread batter in prepared pan. Sprinkle almonds over top.

4. Bake 30 minutes or until set. Cool completely in pan on wire rack. Cut into squares.

Autumn Apple Bars

1 package (15 ounces) refrigerated pie crusts (2 crusts)

1 cup graham cracker crumbs

8 tart cooking apples, peeled and sliced ¼ inch thick (8 cups)

1 cup plus 2 tablespoons granulated sugar, divided

2½ teaspoons ground cinnamon, divided

¼ teaspoon ground nutmeg

1 egg white

1 cup powdered sugar

1 to 2 tablespoons milk

½ teaspoon vanilla

1. Preheat oven to 350°F. Roll out one pie crust to 15X10-inch rectangle on lightly floured surface. Place in ungreased 15X10-inch sheet pan.

2. Sprinkle graham cracker crumbs over dough; layer apple slices over crumbs. Combine 1 cup granulated sugar, 1½ teaspoons cinnamon and nutmeg in small bowl; sprinkle over apples.

3. Roll out remaining pie crust to 15X10-inch rectangle; place over apple layer. Beat egg white in small bowl until foamy; brush over top crust. Combine remaining 2 tablespoons granulated sugar and remaining 1 teaspoon cinnamon in separate small bowl; sprinkle over crust.

4. Bake 45 minutes or until lightly browned. Cool completely in pan on wire rack.

5. Combine powdered sugar, 1 tablespoon milk and vanilla in small bowl; stir until smooth. Add additional milk, if necessary, to reach desired consistency. Drizzle over bars.

Buttery Oatmeal Turtle Bars

CRUST
- 1 cup all-purpose flour
- 1 cup old-fashioned oats
- ¾ cup packed brown sugar
- ¼ teaspoon salt
- ½ cup (1 stick) unsalted butter, softened
- 1½ cups whole pecans

TOPPING
- ⅔ cup packed brown sugar
- ½ cup (1 stick) unsalted butter
- ½ teaspoon vanilla
- 4 ounces semisweet or milk chocolate

1. Preheat oven to 350°F.

2. For crust, combine flour, oats, ¾ cup brown sugar and salt in medium bowl; mix well. Cut in ½ cup butter with pastry blender or fingers until coarse crumbs form. Press mixture firmly onto bottom of ungreased 13X9-inch baking pan. Sprinkle with pecans.

3. For topping, combine ⅔ cup brown sugar and ½ cup butter in medium heavy saucepan. Bring to a boil over medium heat; boil 1 minute. Remove from heat; stir in vanilla. Pour evenly over pecans.

4. Bake 15 to 18 minutes or until topping is bubbly. Break chocolate into 1-inch chunks. Sprinkle evenly over caramel layer. Bake 1 minute or until melted.

5. Using tip of knife, gently swirl chocolate into topping. Cool slightly; refrigerate until set. Cut into bars.

Coconut Fruit Bars

CRUST

- 1 cup all-purpose flour
- 3 tablespoons powdered sugar
- ¼ teaspoon salt
- ½ cup (1 stick) unsalted butter, softened

FILLING

- 1 cup granulated sugar
- ¼ cup all-purpose flour
- ½ teaspoon baking powder
- ¼ teaspoon salt
- 2 eggs
- ½ teaspoon coconut extract
- ½ teaspoon vanilla
- ¾ cup sliced almonds
- ¾ cup flaked sweetened coconut
- ½ cup chopped dried apricots*
- ½ cup chopped dried tart cherries*

Spray knife with nonstick cooking spray to prevent sticking while chopping, or cut with kitchen scissors.

1. Preheat oven to 350°F. Grease 11X7-inch baking pan.

2. For crust, combine 1 cup flour, powdered sugar and ¼ teaspoon salt in small bowl; mix well. Beat butter in large bowl with electric mixer at medium speed until creamy. Gradually add flour mixture at low speed, beating just until blended. Press evenly into prepared pan. Bake 18 to 22 minutes or until set and lightly browned. Cool on wire rack.

3. For filling, combine granulated sugar, ¼ cup flour, baking powder and ¼ teaspoon salt in large bowl; mix well. Stir in eggs, coconut extract and vanilla; mix well. Stir in almonds, coconut, apricots and cherries; mix until evenly blended. Spread evenly over crust.

4. Bake 24 to 28 minutes until set and golden brown. Cool completely in pan on wire rack. Cut into bars.

Orange Cappuccino Brownies

MAKES 2 TO 3 DOZEN BROWNIES

¾ cup (1½ sticks) unsalted butter

2 ounces semisweet chocolate, coarsely chopped

2 ounces unsweetened chocolate, coarsely chopped

1¾ cups granulated sugar

1 tablespoon instant espresso powder or instant coffee granules

3 eggs

¼ cup orange-flavored liqueur

2 teaspoons grated orange peel

1 cup all-purpose flour

1 package (12 ounces) semisweet chocolate chips

2 tablespoons shortening

1. Preheat oven to 350°F. Grease 13X9-inch baking pan or line with parchment paper.

2. Melt butter and chocolate in large heavy saucepan over low heat, stirring constantly. Stir in sugar and espresso powder. Remove from heat; cool slightly. Add eggs, beating well after each addition. Stir in liqueur and orange peel. Add flour; stir just until blended. Spread batter in prepared pan. Bake 25 to 30 minutes or until center is firm to the touch. Place pan on wire rack.

3. Combine chocolate chips and shortening in small microwavable bowl. Microwave on HIGH 1 minute; stir. Microwave at 30-second intervals until chocolate is melted and mixture is smooth. Immediately spread melted chocolate mixture over warm brownies. Cool completely in pan on wire rack. Cut into bars.

Chocolate Walnut Bars

1½ cups all-purpose flour

¾ cup granulated sugar

¾ cup (1½ sticks) cold unsalted butter

1 can (14 ounces) sweetened condensed milk

1 cup semisweet chocolate chips

1 egg

½ teaspoon vanilla

2 cups walnuts, chopped and toasted*

To toast walnuts, spread in single layer on baking sheet. Bake in preheated 350°F oven 8 to 10 minutes or until fragrant, stirring frequently.

1. Preheat oven to 350°F.

2. Combine flour and sugar in large bowl; cut in butter using pastry blender or fingers until mixture resembles coarse crumbs. Press onto bottom of ungreased 13X9-inch baking pan. Bake 20 minutes or until lightly browned.

3. Meanwhile, combine sweetened condensed milk and chocolate chips in medium saucepan. Cook and stir over low heat until smooth. Remove from heat; cool slightly.

4. Add egg and vanilla to chocolate mixture; stir until well blended. Stir in walnuts. Spread chocolate mixture over partially baked crust.

5. Bake 25 minutes or until center is set. Cool completely in pan on wire rack. Cut into bars.

Chewy Pecan Gingersnap Triangles

MAKES 2 DOZEN TRIANGLES

20 gingersnap cookies, broken in half

½ cup (1 stick) unsalted butter, softened

¼ cup granulated sugar

¼ cup packed brown sugar

1 egg, separated

½ teaspoon vanilla

¼ teaspoon salt

1 teaspoon water

1½ cups chopped pecan pieces (6 ounces)

1. Preheat oven to 350°F. Line bottom and sides of 13×9-inch baking pan with foil, leaving 2-inch overhang. Spray foil with nonstick cooking spray.

2. Place gingersnap cookies in food processor; process until crumbs form. (Or place cookies in resealable food storage bag and crush with rolling pin or meat mallet.)

3. Beat butter, granulated sugar, brown sugar, egg yolk and vanilla in medium bowl with electric mixer at medium until well blended. Add cookie crumbs and salt; mix well. Lightly press crumb mixture into bottom of prepared pan to form thin crust.

4. Whisk egg white and water in small bowl. Brush egg white mixture evenly over crust; sprinkle evenly with pecans. Lightly press pecans to adhere to crust.

5. Bake 20 minutes or until lightly browned. Cool completely in pan on wire rack. Use foil handles to remove bars from pan to cutting board. Cut into 3-inch squares; cut squares diagonally in half.

Metric Conversion Chart

VOLUME MEASUREMENTS (dry)

$^1/_8$ teaspoon = 0.5 mL
$^1/_4$ teaspoon = 1 mL
$^1/_2$ teaspoon = 2 mL
$^3/_4$ teaspoon = 4 mL
1 teaspoon = 5 mL
1 tablespoon = 15 mL
2 tablespoons = 30 mL
$^1/_4$ cup = 60 mL
$^1/_3$ cup = 75 mL
$^1/_2$ cup = 125 mL
$^2/_3$ cup = 150 mL
$^3/_4$ cup = 175 mL
1 cup = 250 mL
2 cups = 1 pint = 500 mL
3 cups = 750 mL
4 cups = 1 quart = 1 L

VOLUME MEASUREMENTS (fluid)

1 fluid ounce (2 tablespoons) = 30 mL
4 fluid ounces ($^1/_2$ cup) = 125 mL
8 fluid ounces (1 cup) = 250 mL
12 fluid ounces (1$^1/_2$ cups) = 375 mL
16 fluid ounces (2 cups) = 500 mL

WEIGHTS (mass)

$^1/_2$ ounce = 15 g
1 ounce = 30 g
3 ounces = 90 g
4 ounces = 120 g
8 ounces = 225 g
10 ounces = 285 g
12 ounces = 360 g
16 ounces = 1 pound = 450 g

DIMENSIONS

$^1/_{16}$ inch = 2 mm
$^1/_8$ inch = 3 mm
$^1/_4$ inch = 6 mm
$^1/_2$ inch = 1.5 cm
$^3/_4$ inch = 2 cm
1 inch = 2.5 cm

OVEN TEMPERATURES

250°F = 120°C
275°F = 140°C
300°F = 150°C
325°F = 160°C
350°F = 180°C
375°F = 190°C
400°F = 200°C
425°F = 220°C
450°F = 230°C

BAKING PAN SIZES

Utensil	Size in Inches/Quarts	Metric Volume	Size in Centimeters
Baking or Cake Pan (square or rectangular)	8×8×2	2 L	20×20×5
	9×9×2	2.5 L	23×23×5
	12×8×2	3 L	30×20×5
	13×9×2	3.5 L	33×23×5
Loaf Pan	8×4×3	1.5 L	20×10×7
	9×5×3	2 L	23×13×7
Round Layer Cake Pan	8×1½	1.2 L	20×4
	9×1½	1.5 L	23×4
Pie Plate	8×1¼	750 mL	20×3
	9×1¼	1 L	23×3
Baking Dish or Casserole	1 quart	1 L	—
	1½ quart	1.5 L	—
	2 quart	2 L	—